The Jester

Leslie Moore

Alpha Editions

This edition published in 2022

ISBN: 9789356318328

Design and Setting By

Alpha Editions

www.alphaedis.com

Email - info@alphaedis.com

As per information held with us this book is in Public Domain.
This book is a reproduction of an important historical work.
Alpha Editions uses the best technology to reproduce historical work
in the same manner it was first published to preserve its original nature.
Any marks or number seen are left intentionally to preserve.

Table of Contents

CHAPTER I CAP AND BELLS	- 1 -
CHAPTER II THE FOOL'S ENTRY	- 8 -
CHAPTER III SWEET BONDAGE	- 16 -
CHAPTER IV A WOMAN'S WILL	- 21 -
CHAPTER V GOOD COMRADESHIP	- 24 -
CHAPTER VI BALDA THE WITCH	- 30 -
CHAPTER VII SANCTUARY	- 36 -
CHAPTER VIII COUNCIL AT SANGDIEU	- 40 -
CHAPTER IX THE CASTING OF THE NET	- 45 -
CHAPTER X WITHERED ROSES	- 49 -
CHAPTER XI OUTCASTE	- 55 -
CHAPTER XII THE WANDERER	- 60 -
CHAPTER XIII CASTLE SYRTES	- 64 -
CHAPTER XIV THE QUEST	- 71 -
CHAPTER XV SIMON OF THE BEES	- 75 -
CHAPTER XVI ILLUSION	- 82 -
CHAPTER XVII APHORISMS	- 84 -
CHAPTER XVIII THE SAGE	- 91 -

CHAPTER XIX THE CHOICE	- 94 -
CHAPTER XX VIBRATIONS	- 100 -
CHAPTER XXI MOON RITUAL	- 104 -
CHAPTER XXII DEVIL WORSHIP	- 110 -
CHAPTER XXIII ABBOT HILARY	- 116 -
CHAPTER XXIV AT DIEUPORTE	- 122 -
CHAPTER XXV AN ORCHARD EGOIST	- 125 -
CHAPTER XXVI AELRED'S BELIEF	- 130 -
CHAPTER XXVII THE RECLUSE	- 135 -
CHAPTER XXVIII IN THE FOREST	- 141 -
CHAPTER XXIX EASTER EVE AND EASTER MORNING	- 145 -

CHAPTER I

CAP AND BELLS

NICHOL the Jester having left this world for, we trust, a better, and thereto we cry "God rest his soul," Peregrine his son reigned in his stead.

This was in accordance with custom. Six times had cap and bells descended from father to son: we see Peregrine as the seventh inheritor thereto, which, perchance, holds some significance. Pythagorus would doubtless have told us it held much; would have told us we find in seven the last of the limited numbers, a mere step from it to the free vibrations. Also he would have seen double significance in that Peregrine's own name held the same vibration. And who are we to say him nay?

For my part I would no more dream of venturing to gainsay him than I would venture to gainsay the old sage who read the message of the stars at his birth. This sage, finding him born under the third decanate of Sagittarius, with Uranus in the ascendant, and having muttered of houses, and cusps, and aspects, and signs, and I know not what besides,—and if I did would refrain from further enumeration lest I should weary you,—proclaimed him one born to wander, a seeker after that which is not easily found,—of the sign of Sagittarius, and the planet Uranus are antiquarians and alchemists. He gave him also favours from one of high birth, which favours should wither like June roses when picked; gave him sorrow as companion for a space,—though truly there is no mother's son of us knows not that companion for a while,—and the end of his life's journey he saw not. Whereat I, for one, rejoice, since—though I would not venture to gainsay the old sage—I believe that the ordering of a man's destiny lies not with the stars, but with One Who holds the universe in the Hollow of His Hand.

Lisette, wife of Nichol the Jester, gave however full credence to the sage, a credence equal to that she gave to the dogmas of Holy Church, therein showing herself illogical after the manner of women, since our Mother the Church has ever bade us have no dealing with omens, dreams, the riddle of the stars, and such-like fooleries. Despite this, and having given, as we have seen, credulous ear to the sage's prophecy, she named the boy Peregrine.

When first breeched he was costumed as a miniature edition of his sire, half black, half white, in cognizance of the rôle he would later play in truth. The cap surrounded a chubby face, not yet outgrown the solemnity of babyhood. His hand, fat and dimpled, grasped the belled bauble. Borne aloft on his father's shoulder to the great hall, he was set in the midst of the squires and dames,—more particularly the dames, since the squires for the most part were that day following their lord over Exmoor in pursuit of the wild red deer.

They saw in him a pretty enough plaything; found, for a time at least, greater novelty in his solemn silences and rare smiles than in his father's jests. The Lady Clare de Belisle entering with her own child, a girl babe of two summers, touched the tiny jester's cheek with one jewelled finger, commended him for a bonny boy. The two children gazed at each other solemn-eyed, till Isabel, the girl, putting forth her hand was for taking the young jester's bauble from him. Thereat Peregrine clutched it jealously to his breast, having no mind to part with his toy.

"I want," said Isabel, one fat finger pointed towards the treasure clutched by the scowling boy. That was the way with Isabel in childhood as in later years, knowing what she desired she hesitated not to demand it, and obtain it by whatever means came best to hand.

It is not becoming that the son of a Jester should deny the desire of his Lady's daughter. Nichol, the dames, my Lady even, were prepared for insistence, a ruthless seizing of the treasure from the baby grasp; when suddenly and without compulsion, the child's mien changed. Of his own accord he tendered the bauble to Isabel.

She took it, smiling. Even babes can be gracious when their wish is granted. For a moment she held it examining it with curiosity, a curiosity soon satiated, since after a brief space she held it in a listless hand, tendered it again.

"I don't like it."

Peregrine backed away from her. Perhaps—in fact I am sure—there was reproach in his blue eyes. So for a moment they stood. Then Isabel cast the bauble upon the ground. And herein some may read an omen. The squires and dames laughed; my Lady murmured a gentle word of chiding; Nichol picked up the bauble; but Peregrine still looked at Isabel.

This, then, was Peregrine's introduction to that society wherein later he was to wear the cap and bells as no mere pastime but in very truth. Nor was it at this time his last appearance therein. For the first few years of his life he played, in a manner, the rôle of zany to his father, gaining thereby much favour. Candour, a virtue allowed both children and fools, was a marked characteristic of Peregrine's. If at moments the recipients of his frank speeches felt a trifle of embarrassment there was always the knowledge that their own blush or wince would presently be superseded by a laugh at the blush or wince of another. This squared all accounts, made the momentary embarrassment worth enduring.

Yet what may well pass as the artlessness of a child, the privilege of a fool, is of other brand from the boy. With the loss of his milk teeth—and he was full late in parting with them—Peregrine's candour began to lose its charm. Outspoken speeches when issuing from between cherry lips and pearls are of different ilk when the pearls are lacking. Herein we see the injustice of the world.

The day came when an outspoken speech of Peregrine's, exceeding apt, perchance of over-candour,—though assuredly a year ago it would have gained him high applause,—was taken in ill part. True, there were some who tittered, yet surreptitiously, feeling the atmosphere somewhat charged with unfriendly omen, an omen none could overlook, seeing that it emanated from the guest of note who sat frowning at the insouciant Peregrine. Had the guest been of less importance it is possible the affair might have been settled by a slight rebuke, but with her rank and dignity in view no such flimsy method was of avail.

Peregrine was dismissed the hall wherein he had been a petted favourite since his first breeching; and, before being deprived of cap and bells, was breeched—and soundly—after other fashion, the distinguished guest having made it evident that the smart of her wounded feelings could only be eased by the smarting of Peregrine's small body.

Sore and sobbing he sought his mother, wept out his woes, his perplexities, his hot face buried in her lap. Thus with pain of body, though with but dim realization of mind, Peregrine first became acquainted with the injustice of the world.

For a time Peregrine saw the hall no more. Clad after the ordinary manner of his kind he kept out of the way of the noblesse, the gentry, ill at ease when he by chance crossed their path, found what human companionship he would among the servitors alone,—excepting always that of his father and mother, in whose company he at all times found pleasure.

He took now to frequenting the woods and moors which lay around the castle. Lying on the heather, its scent and the scent of the golden gorse warm and fragrant in his nostrils, he would gaze over the surrounding country, see the blue channel below him gleaming in the sunlight, the Welsh coast dim and hazy beyond, look northwards to the small town nestling at the foot of the hill which rises some eight hundred feet above it.

Roaming the woods he would watch for the first hint of Spring in the swelling buds of the larch trees, would rejoice in the faint shimmer of green flung over them when she first shows a shy face, would seek among brown leaves scattered on the ground for the pale primrose, the delicate windflower, the fragile wood sorrel with its tiny white petals lightly veined in mauve. Here he learned of the ways of the wild creatures of nature, rather than the ways of men, and found them more to his liking. What we give that shall we receive, so are we told, though verily there are times when the giving will appear to outweigh all receipts. Possibly this is because we look to reward to follow hard upon bestowal, trust not to the finding after many days. Here in the woods, however, Peregrine found swift reward. The love he bestowed upon the woodland creatures gained him their love in return. The birds would feed from his hand, the animals brought their young to play at his feet; confidence between them and him reached a very pretty note of harmony.

Wandering further afield he would watch the red deer which in daylight found hiding-place in distant combes, see them in moonlight moving in great herds across the moor. In the combes he would go boldly up to them, feed them with pieces of coarse bread, and bunches of freshly pulled grass. Only in the mating season he left them alone, knowing the wild jealousy of the stag.

When, as frequently happened, he heard the huntsman's horn, caught a glimpse of hounds, horses, and their riders in full cry, he would clench his brown fists, his young jaw set in a grim line, his whole body a-quiver with rage. Even so might a man feel who saw his friend hunted to his death.

Once when the harriers were out after a hare, and being close on her heels, the frighted creature, seeing Peregrine, turned, crouching at his feet. In a twinkling he had her in his arms, swarmed, still holding her, up an oak, whence hidden in the topmost branches, too slender to bear aught but a boy's weight, he heard angry baying at the tree's base. Presently up came the huntsmen. There was a colloquy, a debating. The foliage was too thick to allow of Peregrine being perceived, perched as he was aloft, one arm entwining a bough, the other clutching the hare, which for the moment lay panting, too frightened for struggle. It is not in the nature of things for hares to climb trees; nor was the actual occurrence one likely to dawn on the unaided imagination. Baffled, perplexed, the huntsmen stood among the baying harriers, scratching their heads, flicking their boots with their riding crops, swearing meanwhile each after his own particular form and fancy. And the dogs, who might have told them the manner of the happening, being dumb of human speech but bayed the louder. A hole in the oak's trunk some four feet or so from the ground offered a solution, an unlikely one enough, yet at this juncture better than none. Madam Hare, so they asseverated among themselves, had sprung for the hole and by ill chance for their sport had reached it. No doubt she was now crouched within the hollow of the oak. To get her out was impossible, short of felling the tree; and in very sooth she had found a worse death within that prison than the quick end the dogs would have made of her.

Yet, in spite of seeing Madam Hare as escaped from their clutches, a victim of a slow death by starvation, they still lingered, muttering, jabbering, swearing; the dogs still making loud din, causing Peregrine's heart to beat with fear, knowing not of the hole in the tree which had doubtless saved his skin, and the life of the trembling creature in his arm. The weight of the animal was no light one, and his muscles began to suffer cramp. Feeling extremity at hand he put up a small prayer, which possibly was heard by Saint Francis, seeing he had once rescued a like creature from the hounds. Whether it was the advocacy of the prayer, or whether the huntsmen were weary of their sojourn beneath the tree, you may settle as it best pleases you; for my part I will maintain that the Saint himself drew them away, caused them to call off the dogs, and ride baulked of their prey away from wood and moor.

Silence had fallen for the space of some ten or fifteen minutes before Peregrine thought safe to descend; and in that the hare had lain quiet so long we may likewise see the hand of the gentle Saint. Twenty yards or so away from the tree, clear from the scent of the dogs, Peregrine deposited his burden upon the ground. A moment she crouched while his hand caressed her soft fur, then leaping, vanished down the glade.

Yet this freedom of wood and moorland, this sojourning with wild creatures, that I have shown you, belonged in main to Peregrine's boyhood. As he grew older it was not thought well, by those who had a say in the matter, that he should roam in idleness. Those who eat bread must needs earn it after some fashion, save those who are born, as the saying is, with a silver spoon in the mouth. Peregrine after a while found his hours of roaming curtailed. Armourer, falconer, grooms, alike pressed him into service. No special calling allotted him in view of the one rôle he should later play—though if the truth be known he looked to it with but little favour—he became the server of many. This, as may be imagined, irked him somewhat. He had no mind to await any man's behest, yet mind or not he found it must needs be done. Being no fool he brought, then, to his tasks what good grace he might. Besides his work with armourer, falconer, and grooms, he learned to play the tabor, and had a very pretty skill thereon.

Of these years I have little to record. They were in the main uneventful. Their chief incident as far as Peregrine was concerned, and one of deep sorrow to him, was his mother's death. That was a sorrow which lay heavy for many a long month, till time at length began imperceptibly to ease the burden of his grief.

Peregrine had come to man's estate, had seen, I take it, four and twenty summers or thereabouts, when Nichol was stricken of the ague which was to end for him this mortal life. Lying gaunt and hollow-eyed on his bed, the cap and bells on an oak chest near, he called his son to him, pointed with one wasted hand towards the motley dress.

"To-morrow, or the next day, you will be wearing it," he said.

Peregrine bowed his head. Finding it ill to lie, even for comfort's sake, in the face of Death, he was silent.

"A jest more often than not holds truth," said Nichol, "yet now, between you and me, the truth may be spoken without need of jest." His eyes, blue like Peregrine's, sought his son's eyes, but Peregrine's were lowered.

"Look at me," said his father.

Peregrine raised his eyes.

"You like not the thought. That I have long known. Yet, what will you? Fate made of me a Jester, as she made a Jester of my father and his sires before me, as she now makes one of you. I accepted my rôle as in the nature of things. With you it is otherwise. Submitting outwardly to the decree of fate, inwardly your spirit rebels. It will be hard for you. The rôle of Jester is no easy one. Dogs are we, waiting with a dog's wistfulness on the smile of our master's lips, the pat of our master's hand. And if, rather than smile and pat, we receive frown and blow, yet may we not bite, since that is of the manner of a cur; nor cringe, since cringing is likewise of a cur. We must accept the frown and blow submissively, should e'en return with wagging tail to fawn upon the hand that struck us; and if we are wise dogs will learn new tricks better suited to please. And the man's heart in us we should drug, if we cannot kill it, lest it grow to torment us. I drugged mine, or tried to. It was, perchance, too strong to kill. Yet for all the drugging there were times when it pulsed less sluggishly. That day when they took the cap and bells from you, when they beat you, poor miserable little fool, I jested my best. Had I not jested I would have flung my bauble in the face of the woman who sat there smiling as your cries reached the hall. And the man's heart suffered torment that day in the dog's body. Yet Jester I was then, Jester I have been since. Now at last I am man, and wholly man. Death, when his shadow touches us, grants us that much solace."

He stopped. Peregrine, kneeling by the bed, found no words.

"Custom," went on Nichol, "is strong upon man; strongest of all, perchance, upon the Jester. Despite our moments of resentment we look for applause. It is our life, our breath. We long for the favour of our master.

I have said we are dogs, and when that is said, all is said. Yet the man's heart may outgrow the dog's body. You will don the motley; you, too, will fawn upon the hand that strikes you; you, too, will watch with wistful eyes on the desire of your master. Yet if, as I fancy, the day dawns when drugs no longer bring their soothing anodyne to your man's heart, when the soul within the motley is a soul in prison, then remember that I now have asked your pardon for the heritage you will accept from me. That is all. Now, son, fetch me a priest."

Of Peregrine's words e'er he went to fulfil his father's last behest, I make no record. They were not intended, as may well be guessed, for you or me to know. When they were spoken he rose from his knees, set out for the Abbey of Our Lady of the Cliff.

CHAPTER II

THE FOOL'S ENTRY

AND so it came to pass that Peregrine again saw the hall, entered thereto garbed once more in cap and bells. Candour, so he decreed, should be far from his lips, having in his mind the memory of a day now some sixteen years old. It was not for these among whom he should pass his time. Guile, art, cynicism, anything but truth should be used wherewith to fashion the jests, the darts of speech which he should throw abroad. A Jester heedless of applause, of frowns, or smiles, thus he saw himself, wise for the moment in his own conceit.

Here you perceive youth, which sees itself strong to venture, disbelieving the prophecies of age. Yet were it not for venturesome youth we may well believe that little would be attained. The babe, who first totters on unsteady feet, may well lack the qualms, the anxieties of the mother who sees the fall imminent. Had the babe her mental tremors methinks there is no mother's son of us would learn aught but to crawl.

Peregrine stood by the window in the great hall. He found himself alone. Rain, a thin mist of a rain, fell ceaselessly, insidiously from a leaden sky. The cloyed earth accepted it patiently. There was no joy in the acceptance, no eager thirst as for silver showers streaming downwards. Sodden and satiated it longed for the benign rays of the sun to awaken the half-drowned life within its bosom.

Peregrine looking across the park to the further reaches of the moorland saw it through a grey mist. The outlook accorded well with his mood. It lacked colour, buoyancy. The future appeared as skeleton as the bare branches of the trees flung against the sullen sky. If Nature's spring were at hand she hid her face well. Mentally he had no glimpse of her, nor looked to have any. A morbid mood for a man you may well say, yet this was Peregrine's at the moment.

Turning from the window he scanned the hall, his eyes roving from inlaid floor to domed ceiling, from arched doorway to carved fireplace. The daylight was waning. Shadows loomed in the corners, were flung trembling on the walls by the firelight,—tongued flames among great logs. The light caught the blazon of the house of Belisle among the carving of the overmantel.—*On a field argent an inescutcheon azure set within an orle of roses gules.*

He looked at it thoughtfully, memory astir. As a child the vivid bit of colour had pleased him as it flashed jewel-like in sunshine or firelight from the sombre shadows of the oak. It pleased his eye now no less, though memory pricking touched the old wound anew.

To him in this pensive mood entered a page, a slim lad in blue and silver. Peregrine engrossed in thought heard no sound till:

"Ahem!" coughed the page.

Peregrine started, looked up, met a pair of grey eyes, mischief lurking in their depths, saw a smooth-skinned, square-faced lad, wide-mouthed, with tip-tilted nose.

"Craving your pardon for breaking in upon your meditations," quoth the lad with mock respect, "but the Lady Isabel desires your presence."

Peregrine, returning to matters of the moment, experienced a heart beat. Here was his stage call, and his part by no means well-conned as yet. Save at a distance he had not set eyes upon the Lady Isabel since childhood, sole mistress now of the house of Belisle, since the Lady Clare, her mother, had been laid to rest. The Lord Robert de Belisle, her father, was in Gascony with his King subduing a rebellion.

"And she has sent you to demand my presence?" asked Peregrine lazily, his inward tremor well controlled.

"Since I am here," grinned the boy.

"Where is she?" demanded Peregrine, less desirous of knowing than wishful to gain a moment's respite.

"In the west chamber among her women," replied the boy. "She is—weary." A pause preceded the last word.

Peregrine lifted his tabor from the broad sill of the window.

"Take me to her," he said.

Crossing the hall and mounting the stairs the boy eyed Peregrine, gave him the close scrutiny of childhood, summed up what he found there, and I fancy found it not amiss for all that it is not usual to pay a vast respect to fools. Peregrine caught the lad's eye upon him.

"Well, what do you make of me?" he smiled.

The boy flushed scarlet from brow to chin. Having caught a glimpse of the man beneath the motley words halted on his tongue.

"Your name?" asked Peregrine still smiling.

"Antony Philip Delamore," stuttered the lad. "They call me Pippo."

"Pippo," echoed Peregrine thoughtfully. And the boy heard the name pleasantly from his lips.

The stairs mounted they passed along a corridor, paused at an alcove curtain-hung with tapestry. Here Pippo, entering first, held aside the heavy draperies.

"Madam, the Jester awaits your pleasure."

A voice smooth, flexible, yet holding, one would say, a ring of metal rather than a hint of silkiness, replied:

"Well, let him enter."

Peregrine stepped across the threshold, and Pippo let the curtain fall behind him.

In the room lighted by candles, a woman sat beside the fireplace. Her dress was of crimson silk, a splash of colour against the darkness of the oak chair, and in the shadows of the room. She was tall and very slight, yet you could not call her thin. Her skin was of ivory whiteness. Her brow, low and broad, was framed in masses of dark hair glinting with vivid red lights. You caught the gleam of pearls among its darkness. Towards the chin the face narrowed sharply. The mouth, subtle-lipped, showed a hint of snowy teeth. The eyes brown, lustrous, with the blue whites of a child's eyes, looked from beneath level brows towards the curtain.

Peregrine saw her eyes.

With her were her four women,—Mary Chester, the oldest, steady-eyed, smooth-haired, common sense well mingled with devoutness; Leonora Ashton, a well grown girl, built to be the mother of sons, healthy in mind and body alike; Monica Cardew, a willowy slip of a girl, dreamy, with little thought beyond her embroideries and her rosary; and last Brigid Carlisle, square-faced, merry, something boyish. Well-favoured women the first three, each after her own fashion, Brigid alone having no pretension to looks, though a pleasant face you would have found it, yet the beauty of the three maids dimmed beside that of the mistress.

Nature as a rule gives discreetly. Giving features she deems to have done well if she withholds colouring, giving colouring she withholds features. Giving brains she often withholds form, giving form she may pay but scant attention to brains. Of virtue I make no mention seeing it is a gift of grace rather than appertaining solely to Nature. Yet now and again, at rare moments truly, Nature becomes prodigal of her gifts, bestows open-handed. Thus her gifts to Isabel de Belisle. I have given you but the outline, you may fill in the detail, and add thereto that most subtle, elusive, and unaccountable of her gifts,—charm, personality, fascination—call it what you will.

Peregrine, I have told you, saw her eyes. Then remembering her presence bowed low before her.

Isabel scanned him, a quick glance, very comprehensive. Since we have here been dealing with Nature's gifts we may well see those she has accorded our Jester. A lean-limbed man he was, tall, and very straight. The face, surrounded by the cap half black, half white, was bronzed with sun and open air. The hair hidden beneath it one might well guess to be dark, judging from the slight shadow on shaven lip and chin. The nose was straight, the nostrils sensitive. The eyes, black-lashed, were of an extraordinary blueness. Looking in his face you were aware of vivid colour, and saw that it lay in his eyes. The pupils were very black. The mouth, sensitive as the nostrils, was firm-lipped. The chin, square, was set at a fine angle with the jaw. Seeking for character you would have read determination in the line.

Isabel was not the only woman who scanned him. The four maids had their glances ready,—Mary Chester's brief but sure; Leonora's calm, somewhat indifferent; Monica's swift, timid, eyes falling again to the frame of her embroidery; Brigid's frank, boyish almost. But Peregrine's eyes were still upon Isabel.

Isabel looking found novelty. Nor was it merely the novelty in a new-comer, a novelty enhanced by dreary weather, enforced sojourn within doors. In outward form she saw a Jester, good-looking enough, but merely a Jester such as his sire and grandsires before him. Yet for a brief space, swift as the tongued lightning which shoots across the darkened sky, she saw something more than mere fool. And having seen it she perceived in the fool the cloak to a riddle, a riddle perchance worth the solving. Yet she gave no hint of having seen.

"Your name, Sir Jester?" she demanded, her eyes now upon the fire, speaking of set purpose without looking at him, as one may speak to a servant.

"Peregrine, Madam."

"Peregrine?" she dwelt on the syllables. "A bird?"

"A species of hawk, Madam."

"Then a bird of prey?"

"Maybe; yet swift of flight, a wanderer."

"Ah! And were you named for prey, flight, or wanderer?"

Peregrine lifted his shoulders, the merest suspicion of a shrug. "The last, so my mother told me."

"Yet you have not wandered far, nor are likely to do so."

"True, Madam; yet you speak now of the body."

"The body?"

"The spirit may soar aloft, wander in realms of fancy. No man but the owner may clip the wings of that bird."

"You speak seriously for a Jester."

"Serious words, Madam, cloak light fancies. Light words cloak serious fancies. Therefore you perceive my fancies, being light of wing, can soar."

"Ah!" She threw him a swift glance, read something sombre in his eyes; remembered, since a woman's heart should surely hold some thought for others, that death's hand had but lately touched one near to him.

Peregrine read her glance; had no mind for pity in that direction. Death had come as a good friend to his sire, had flung the cell door open. Yet how to turn her thought? How act the part it was his to play? Fate had indeed flung the rôle upon him, garbed his body while poorly equipping his tongue. In this he perceived her irony. Seeking for words his hand touched his tabor.

"Madam, I know a song."

"But one?" Her voice held a hint of mockery.

"For the moment."

"A merry song? A sad song?"

"Madam, it will accord with the mood of the listener, therefore I will term it neither a merry song, nor a sad song, but an adaptable song."

She leaned back in her chair. "An unusual song. Let us hear it."

Peregrine struck a couple of chords on the tabor, then in a voice not large, but a sweet barytone, he sang:

Ah, what it is to dream

Know ye, who seek to deem

Your way a path more bright

Than that it now doth seem;

More grand of sight, more bathed in light.

Ah, what it is to dream!

If thou dost e'er desire
To seek sweet fancy's fire,
To warm at her soft flame,
Repent not of the hire,
Nor whence it came, nor count it blame
If thou dost e'er desire.

Nor seek to close thine eyes,
But take this good advice
And quest with willing heart.
For they are truly wise
Who bear the smart of fire apart.
Nor seek to close thine eyes.

And shrink not from the fire
If thou hast true desire
Through pain to win thy day.
Shake from thy feet the mire,
The mud of clay gained by the way,
And shrink not from the fire.

So shall thou find thy goal,
And finding gain thy soul.
Thy dreaming was not all;
It asked a lesser toll,
A toll so small. Then came the call.
So shall thou find thy goal.

The song ended a silence fell on the room. Mary Chester had heard it very sanely, the words lost for the most part in the melody that accompanied them. Leonora, dreaming, saw the goal of motherhood, though as yet distant. Monica pictured some peaceful cloister, heard the sweet tones of the Angelus. Brigid, half-smiling, sighed; saw, I fancy, further than did the others.

As for Isabel, she looked at the fire. Pippo, lying on the hearth, looked from her to Peregrine.

"Whose are the words?" asked Isabel.

"Madam, they come from realms of fancy."

"Your own?"

"Those wherein I have occasionally wandered."

"Find you many such songs there?"

"Now and again. They are, however, often elusive, escaping as soon as perceived."

Isabel turned from the fire, looked full at him. She gave him now a smile, rare with her, though Peregrine was not to know that. His heart beat hotly.

"Methinks," she said, "you are poet rather than Jester."

The colour rushed to Peregrine's face. Memory of his resolution surged towards him, yet was it driven back by the smile that trembled on her lips.

"Madam, I—" he stammered.

Isabel misunderstood the hesitation. She had seen his sire wince with the new jest ready on his tongue. Here was no jest ready, and strangely enough she would cloak the deficiency.

"I—I am not displeased." The words fell softly from her lips.

And at that laughter sprang to Peregrine's throat, a flash of mockery to his eyes, though he replied gravely enough and meekly, "Madam, I am at all times what you would desire me."

"Ah!" breathed Isabel watching him. Then very sweetly, "Now I see in you courtier, yet I would have you poet; therefore, sir poet, sing again."

And Peregrine sang.

Some hour or so later, Peregrine departed, Isabel asked carelessly of her women:

"What think you of our Jester?"

"A very proper man," quoth Brigid demurely.

"He has a sweet voice," ventured Monica timidly.

"He differs from his sire," mused Leonora.

Mary Chester alone was silent.

"And you?" asked Isabel, looking directly at her.

"Madam, I have no opinion," replied Mary; and took herself to task for the lie.

CHAPTER III

SWEET BONDAGE

SPRING that year made battle royal with cold winds. Together they fought for the mastery. Yet where they gained in strength she gained in insistence. Driven away she yet returned again and again, till at length they were weary of the fight, and fled before her to return no more.

The victory hers she reigned supreme and triumphant, flung her snowy mantle over fruit trees, kissed to full awakening the flowers in copse and field, roused to chorus of warblings the birds' song in the hedges. Knowing her reign late and soon to pass to that of summer she lost no moment of it once established. The south and west winds, now her subjects, sang softly among the trees and grasses at her bidding. The sun, king of all, crowned his reigning queen.

Peregrine sat in the castle garden at the foot of the white sundial which stood at the edge of the velvet grass sward. Around him were flower-beds brilliant with colour. Here were masses of small purple campanula covering the stone border between flower-bed and flagged path; clumps of anemones many-hued, named for St. Brigid; narcissi golden-eyed trembling in the soft air; forget-me-nots blue as the sky or Our Lady's robe; scillas deeper dyed; tulips chalice-shaped, gold, crimson, and white,—a very riot of colour, gay as the sweet mad call of spring.

Beyond lay the park, the trees clean and fresh in their vesture of new leaves; and beyond that again the open spaces of the moorland. Peregrine, looking thereat, saw its freedom, remembered his own. A prisoner now, he laughed, yet without bitterness. Ten short weeks to change a man, yet he found himself changed.

Peregrine set himself to think. Yet this he found no easy task. He could see himself as he was ten weeks agone, fancied the mental image as clear-cut as a cameo, a good likeness withal. He could see himself as he was now, the outlines dimmed truly, blurred by some curious mist of thought, yet sufficiently clear to know that here was a different man from the sharp-cut cameo. To the change, the manner of its happening, he found it no easy task to bring clear thought. Once a freeman scorning all thought of thraldom, now a prisoner exulting in his bonds. That the bonds which held him differed from those that had held his sire he was very certain. Custom had bound his sire, he had his own word for it. Here was no custom to hold him, but bonds infinitely sweeter, light yet inflexible as iron. He would not be free of them if he could.

What was he? A prisoner in very sooth. Yet more,—a Jester who failed to jest; a man seeking for art, for guile, wherein to hide his heart, yet clothing it ever in truth, though truth carved to poetic fancy.

"Dogs are we!" so had cried his sire. No dog was he to fawn and cringe at the foot of his mistress, but in very sooth a man kneeling in adoration at his lady's shrine. And as he was, so she accepted him, this Jester who could not jest. She saw the man beneath the fool, and stooping from her heights recognized his manhood. Even so might the Gracious Mother of God bend from Heaven to a suppliant son of earth. There was no hint of blasphemy in his thought; in his very manhood he was humble.

You see in him a man who had had no thought for women. Two only had held his love,—his mother, at whose knee in childhood he had prayed, and that other Mother to whom his prayers had been addressed, "*Sancta Maria, Mater Dei, ora pro nobis peccatoribus, nunc et in hora mortis nostræ.*"

Therefore he brought to his lady a very clean heart, a very humble heart, one which in all childlikeness accepted her favours, though warm with the strength of a man's devotion it sang a man's praises in her honour. You must not think that he lifted his eyes one whit higher than the hem of her robe; she was to him a very queen, himself the humblest of her subjects. Yet he knew himself now as man, and no fool, his adoration clean and strong, no hint of the fawner in his attitude.

That the knowledge brought him joy you may well believe. His heart was attuned to the joyous note of spring. Sun, the flowering earth, the soft winds, all were to him but symbols of his happiness, portraying for him his lady's praises. Looking back on his first meeting with her he still felt a flush of shame that he had momentarily doubted her truth, had spoken words that held a note of irony. For that he struck his breast, cried "*Mea culpa*," saw himself the fool his garb set forth. Truth incarnate in woman, so he saw her now, loftily enshrined beside his mother, the shrine I think very near to that of the Mother of God. Kneeling afar at Mass he saw her bend her head in adoration, rejoiced to think they were at one in this great Act of Worship. The whiteness of his love we may well believe lifted him nearer God.

Having, then, some hint of his mood you will know that Peregrine sitting by the sundial found the morning very fair. Having mused, and finding it hard to say by what precise steps he had reached his present goal, he turned from musing, content merely that here he was. Light of heart he looked across the park, saw the shadows lying still and blue beneath the trees, saw the purple outline of the moorland, heard a lark pouring forth exuberant song from the cloudless sky.

At the further end of the grass sward, on a stone bench, Brigid was sitting with Mary Chester. Embroidery, as their custom was, occupied their fingers, or it would be safer to say that Mary's were occupied thereby. Brigid for the most part held her needle idly, her eyes more often roving to the motionless figure by the sundial than bent upon her work.

"Methinks," she said suddenly, breaking a long silence, "that the Lady Isabel favours our present Jester." Head on one side she surveyed the distant figure meditatively, unashamedly.

"The Lady Isabel is gracious to all," said Mary sedately, her eyes upon her embroidery.

"Hmm." Brigid's eyes twinkled. Elbow on knee, chin in cupped hand, she cast a side-long look at Mary. "And will you be recording that small speech at confession."

Mary flushed. "I do not understand," she responded.

"No?" quizzed Brigid. "Oh, Mary, methought you were a truthful woman. And here within the space of one minute you have twice—Oh, fie upon you!"

Mary, her lips folded upon each other, stitched at her embroidery.

"I wonder," mused Brigid, unheeding her companion's silence, "just what our dear mistress intends."

Still Mary was silent.

"You see," pursued Brigid, "you know her, and I know her, and methinks her present mood is dangerous for the peace of mind of our friend yonder. Just how far will she lead him? Just how far will she let him feel her power? Ah me, had I her looks instead of the half-hearted dower Dame Nature has bestowed on me, methinks willy nilly the maid would enter the field with the mistress, and should the maid gain the day I'll warrant the awakening would be less rude to the sleeping fool. Mary, a word in your ear. Melikes that young man."

Mary raised her eyes from her embroidery. "And that," she remarked quietly, "is the truest word you've spoken."

"A true word, verily; but I crave leave to omit the superlative. Let me show the truth of the other words, emphasise it since you hesitate to grant it. Therefore firstly, note our knowledge of the Lady Isabel; secondly, her mood dangerous to the peace of mind of our friend yonder; thirdly, the awakening less rude were it left to me. And firstly, secondly, and thirdly holds, I'll warrant, every whit as much truth as lastly. Hence I say again, I omit the superlative, by your leave."

For a moment Mary was still silent. Then she spoke, her voice grave. "You are barely charitable, Brigid; and, methinks, hardly loyal."

Brigid shrugged her shoulders. "As for loyalty, I do not speak in this fashion save to you. And for charity—bah! Were I to divest my speech of all criticism methinks 'twould be as savourless as food without salt and spices, mere pap for babes."

Mary sighed.

"You sigh, and rightly. Mary, it angers me. Man though he is, his rôle is but that of fool,—fool by birth, heritage, and calling. She is as guarded from him as ever was Brunhilde from Siegfried by the ring of fire. He knows it, and she knows it. Yet by the syren song of her she lures him ever nearer. And, if her song continues, one day in madness he will try to pass the barrier of flame. Her song and madness alone will urge him to the attempt. Then the flame will burn him; and I know, yes, I know, she will mock at his wounds." Low and fierce Brigid spoke the last words.

"You let imagination run away with you. You feel too deeply." Mary's words were calm.

Brigid looked straight before her. "Sooner feel too deeply than have a heart of stone. Mary, I'd sooner be dumb than lure men by the syren's song. I'd sooner be featureless with leprosy than drive men mad by the fairness of my face. She is heartless as a stone image, remorseless as a Medusa, a very vampire to—." Brigid broke off; a sidelong glance had shown her Mary's face. "You are shocked? Small wonder. Truth is a very naked lady, and if we drag her from the bottom of her well we should at least garb her in becoming fashion. We will lower her again to the darkness of her well, and herewith change the topic of our discourse. Mark you, how blue the sky is, and look at the white butterfly resting on my anemones yonder. See the quivering of its wings, the darling! 'Tis the first I have seen this year." Gaiety in every note of the words you could not have imagined the passionate utterance of a moment agone.

Mary was silent, tears not far from her eyes.

"What ails you?" asked Brigid solicitously.

Mary smiled wanly. "I liked not the sight of truth," she replied.

"Nor I," averred Brigid. "'Twas ill to drag her from her resting-place. Since she cannot be killed she is best hidden. Let us cry *Deo gratias* that there is a well wherein to hide her. And you and I will dance and smile at the edge thereof; since, verily, save for that or moping, which is ill, we can do nothing."

"Nothing," echoed Mary. "Save pray," she added a moment later, and below her breath.

Brigid caught the words, and her eyes gave assent thereto, if not her lips.

CHAPTER IV

A WOMAN'S WILL

HERE you will have seen two views of the same woman, one from the mountain summit, rarified, enfolded almost in the very air of Paradise; the other at the mountain base, to say the least of the earth earthy. Justice demands that I show you some third view of her, and that as dispassionate as may be. From the three you may chose your own view, see it perhaps from a *via media*.

And here my task is no easy one, since to deal with the many intricacies of the human mind, and above all the mind of a woman, needs first a clear perception, secondly a careful adjustment of values, and lastly a nicety of phrase in setting them forth, that those to whom I would show them may see the truth as I believe it, whatever conclusions they may draw therefrom. Partially to achieve this object is all I can hope for; if I give you a glimpse of the truth it must suffice. The rest I must leave to you, trusting to your imagination, your power to mould from the material I will give you. At least I will endeavour that the material be not too hard cast; plastic as may be you shall have it.

And first, by your leave, I would say this: I write, it is true, of days now some six hundred years old, yet human nature has been human nature from the time of our first parents. It is a melody composed at the beginning of the ages; it is repeated throughout the centuries, the air ever the same, underlying the many variations woven around it.

And now to Isabel. Of her outward seeming I have shown you, in so far as I am able with mere pen to portray what should verily be limned by painter's art. Of herself, the inward woman, there is this to say. She desired power. There, in three words, you will perceive the keynote. That given we will on to the further composition. It is by no means certain how far she knew that she desired it. We desire air that we may live and breathe, yet we are not always seeking it, since it is ever with us; it surrounds us, and we accept it with no thought on our own part. Let it be withdrawn and we are conscious of the lack, go forth to seek it. Power was then to Isabel as air is to mankind at large. From childhood—babyhood even—it had been hers to command. All had been ready to do her homage, first on account of her beauty, secondly on account of her charm, since charm she had. There were those, truly, who gave her homage somewhat against their own will, drawn thereto mainly by the example of others. Belonging to a court it is ill to stand aloof from the worship the mistress of the court demands, that worship which her courtiers freely accord her. And this reason may well count for thirdly.

Full homage then was done to Isabel; the power she desired was hers for the most part without effort. Peregrine alone denied it to her.

Personally I see in her neither the heights now accorded her by Peregrine, nor the depths her maids saw in her. Had the heights been hers she surely would have been indifferent to the thought that one man alone refused to do her homage; had the depths been hers she would have borne him malice, set herself to conquer and then to slay. But there was not then, I believe, any definite thought of ill towards him. Of later I am none so sure. It was merely the fruit beyond her reach which had excited her desire. Peregrine the Jester, whose presence she had first demanded with the same indifference she had times out of number demanded the presence of his sire, had, from the moment of his entrance, stirred interest in her. She saw in him, as you have already seen, something more than Jester. The perception was elusive enough to bring the interest to full awakening, to set it as it were on the scent of something further to be discovered. She had heard his song, had seen his face, and had read therein, something of a challenge, or perhaps more rightly had seen a barrier thrown down by the man.

"As fool I give you my allegiance," she might have heard him say. "In that rôle you shall exact from me your due to the uttermost farthing. One iota beyond you shall never gain."

In imagery she had seen him standing aloof, proud, cold, very sure that as man he would never bend the knee to her. Outwardly his rôle should be as perfect as might be, a very skilled art of play-acting, every entrance exact to time, every word carefully conned, faultlessly delivered. She saw him here forcing her to play the part he would assign to her; to deliver, half unconsciously, the speeches that would bring from him the response he desired to make. The very knowledge that he would have the power to do this drew admiration from her, and I am by no means sure that the admiration was grudging. Yet Jester on the stage, he would be man in the wings, smiling at his own skill, mocking at her. This knowledge tantalized, stung, brought her will swiftly yet lightly to the fray. To my thinking this shows her very shallow: her charm I have never denied.

To the mere onlooker the conflict may well seem ignoble, unworthy one of her degree. Yet she saw it in other fashion. Rank, degree, sank for the time being into abeyance. It became the conflict—though lightly undertaken—for a soul that had denied her power. Ignoble we may well call it for the one who recognised the conflict, yet ignoble in other meaning than her courtiers might have termed it. It would be, too, no open fight with trumpet call to battle, lances displayed. In such she might well see herself worsted. The castle of the man's soul must be approached by soft stealth. Guile must take the place of sword and spear.

And Peregrine had no hint of that which was about to befall; there was the pity of it. Forewarned might have been forearmed. It is very true that his father's words had caused him to enclose his soul within a castle, from which, he held, none should lure it forth. Should one use the terms of parable one might name the castle pride. Without, his soul might have had clearer view of approaching dangers. Within, believing himself secure, he saw not the guile which crept towards the walls.

Yet direct speech rather than parable will best serve us in the pursuance of the matter.

Isabel the woman brought every woman's art—and of these not one was lacking her—to conquer Peregrine the man. You have seen the result. I have not given you the details of the conflict nor will do so. Though truly to call it a conflict when never once was seen the flash of naked steel seems somewhat of an anomaly. Isabel's art in this matter would need great skill to set forth. Perchance after some fashion I might show it you were I so minded, yet will I leave it to your imagination. To know the wiles by which a man's spirit is enslaved is not the most pleasing of knowledge. It certainly holds somewhat of sadness, even possibly of distaste.

Peregrine saw no ill in the enslaving, held himself a willing captive; while Isabel for the moment found pleasure in her captive. Recognizing his capitulation it amused her to reward him with many favours. At the present, too, he interested her. She felt his strength, saw in his mind much that she had not yet fully fathomed. That fact pleased her, left her with the possibility of discovery. The joy in the possession of an empty casket, however fair it may be exteriorly, soon palls. One containing much has ever interest. Its contents may be examined at leisure, there is ever that to be found, probably the unexpected, possibly treasure.

You see now how matters stand at the moment. Therefore we will on with the further story.

CHAPTER V

GOOD COMRADESHIP

PIPPO the Page had struck up a friendship with Peregrine the Jester. It had been, I take it, a case of friendship at first sight. A merry youngster was Pippo, saucy after the manner of boys, yet winning for all that. He alone of the court was no slave to Isabel; he did her bidding as it behooved him, yet indifferent to her charms, while she for her part saw in him a very child, not worth her conquest. Later we might hear a different tale.

Pippo had much the same love for the open as had Peregrine in boyhood, and still had for that matter. Yet Pippo's rambles had taken him but seldom beyond the garden and the park. Now, with Peregrine as guide, the two frequently escaped from the more cultured enclosure, made for the woods, the moorlands. Here Pippo learned to see with new eyes, and truly spring is the most welcome season for the learning.

With Peregrine, then, for master, with the fair earth for school, with sweet springtime for the hour, Pippo made vast progress in conning Nature's book. Under this master's tuition it ever held for the boy something truly akin to magic. With unerring divination he had been led to the hollows where the first primrose bloomed, where the first wind-flower swayed its fragile head in the breeze, and this long before the majority of mortals had a hint of blossoming and burgeoning. Later, together they had gazed at the marvel of cup-shaped nest in forked branch or sunny bank, seen therein the eggs blue or mottled brown as the case might be.

Once in the earlier hours of their friendship, it being then, I fancy, not eight days old, the two had fallen in with an aged shepherd, one blowy evening of sleet and rain. Together they had gone a-lambing with him, scouring the darkling fields for the scattered ewes, their ears alert to the cry of the new-born lambs. Here Peregrine had been the surest guide, the quickest to catch the cry of the life new-born. Once started on their work they had remained at it throughout the night. By good fortune rather than good management their absence from the Castle went undetected; yet it was a matter not to be repeated, since the next day Pippo's eyes were heavy with sleep, his brain too drowsy for his duties, whereby he incurred, and not unnaturally, his mistress's displeasure. The arduous task consolidated their friendship. It was a friendship wherein, if there was unbounded admiration on the boy's side, there was something very akin to gratitude on the man's.

Yet the greatest wonder of all in Pippo's eyes was the way of Peregrine with the wild creatures of wood and field. To see the birds come at his call, perch on hand and shoulder, sing therefrom as from a very post of vantage, to watch the dormice, the squirrels awakened from their winter sleep come fearlessly up to him, this indeed was marvel, and marvel to be held in secret bond between them. There was half the joy of it. None but they two knew of their sweet intimacy with Nature's special creatures, those on whom no man had laid the lightest touch of civilization.

Peregrine, too, was a wonderful *raconteur* of tales, ofttimes in verse, ever bathed in fancy. He could translate to the boy's enraptured ears the song the thrush sang to his mate in the golden morning hours, the secrets whispered by the wind as it moved among the fir trees, or through the rushes by the margin of some brook,—very children both of them in mind, with hearts as young as the sweet springtime around them.

One April evening the two sat together on a grassy hillside. Behind them was a copse of hollies, firs, and beeches, a copse of deep undergrowth and green moss. On its margin stood a cherry tree, the wealth of its snowy blossoms backgrounded by a holly bush. Pippo had robbed the tree of a portion of its wealth. It lay beside him in long graceful boughs burdened with white flowers and tender pink-brown leaves. To the left on the southern slope of the hill were massed primroses, and early bluebells, pushing forth among spiked leaves. Scattered at their feet and adown the grassy hill were cuckoo-flowers, their tiny petals most faintly tinged with pinkish purple. Before them lay the channel, blue in the luminous haze which hung over land and water.

"The swallows have returned," quoth Peregrine, as propped on elbow he gazed out to sea.

"Where?" demanded Pippo staring around him.

"They are not here at the moment," laughed Peregrine. "I saw them this morning from my chamber window passing in flocks across the sky."

"Ah!" breathed Pippo envious. "I would that I had seen them."

"Thou wert sleeping, young lazy bones," teased Peregrine.

Pippo gazed straight before him with ardent eyes. "Tomorrow I will awake at daybreak, an hour at least before sunrise," he asseverated.

"And to what end?" demanded Peregrine.

"To look for swallows passing in flocks across the sky," quoth Pippo dreamily. Then, turning, he put a question. "How think you they know, far away beyond England, that here the winter is passed and summer is at hand?"

Peregrine smiled, musing. "How should I give thee an answer as to the thoughts of swallows. Perchance the Blessed Virgin whispers to them."

Pippo eyed him. Albeit he had now known Peregrine some ten weeks and more it came ever fresh to his mind that he spoke on occasions more as woman or monk than man. The men of the court were more ready to take the name of God and His Son on their lips in light oath than speak with tenderness of Our Lady and the Saints. The boy saw in this fashion something of a sign of manhood, in which he found Peregrine strangely lacking. Yet noting the virile strength of the man, the firm swelling of his muscles beneath the close hose and tunic as he moved to sitting posture on the grass, Pippo saw in him—had his thoughts found clear interpretation—something of an anomaly. He had already endured some light mockery for his friendship with the Jester, which—though bringing a quick flush to his cheek—shook his friendship not at all. The loyalty of a child is a very enduring loyalty.

"Of what thinkest thou?" demanded Peregrine.

"Nothing," returned Pippo untruly.

Peregrine smiled, yawned, stretched his long lean limbs, and rose from the grass. "Let's onward," he said.

Pippo scrambled to his feet. Picking up his spoils of the cherry tree he held them sheaf-like in his arms, a fragrant snowy burden. Together they descended the grassy slope, came through a gap in a hedge, and out into a lane beyond.

For a time they walked in silence. Now and again Peregrine glanced at the boy beside him, his head half hidden in the flower sheaf he bore. It was not the first time that Pippo had borne home cherry blossom in his arms. The flower had become associated in Peregrine's mind with these his days of radiant joy. You see his heart very full of sentiment; also he was young.

They had traversed some mile or so of the lane in this silence, when suddenly to their ears came the shrill yelp of an animal in pain. The yelp was followed by another and yet another, rising to a sound that had in it an almost human shriek of agony.

"Some brute is ill-treating a dog," quoth Peregrine, and he set off at a run, Pippo close at his heels.

A couple of hundred yards further on the road turned sharply to the right to an open space of grass. Standing on the grass was a thick-set swarthy-looking fellow, knotted ash stick in one hand, while swinging from the other was a small mongrel dog, bleeding and broken. The stick was doing deadly work.

"Brute!" cried Pippo his cheeks scarlet. Peregrine's face was white.

The fellow started, the stick falling momentarily idle.

"The cur bit me," he muttered, casting an evil look towards them.

"Knowing you the greater cur." Pippo heard an unaccustomed note in Peregrine's voice.

"Go you into the field," said Peregrine shortly, pointing to a gate. Pippo, hearing the tone of command, scuttled through it like a frightened rabbit.

Yet once through he was all for seeing the turn of matters on the other side the hedge. Cherry blossom deposited on the ground he scrambled to the top of the bank. Clinging to the bushes he peered through.

"Ah!" breathed Pippo, joy in the soft sound.

Bah! he need not have feared for Peregrine's manhood. He hugged himself for glee, thereby nearly slithering backwards down the slippery bank. For the first few seconds the tussle was short and fierce, then actual conflict gave place to naught but well-merited punishment. Peregrine's heart had flamed to a white heat of fury. Five minutes later he flung the fellow free. With an oath the man slunk off staggering adown the way the two had come.

Peregrine crossed to the small bundle of palpitating pain by the ditch side. Pippo saw his face. He slipped down from the bank, his heart beating hotly. He heard now what had before escaped him, the small shuddering moans of pain. Then there was another sound.

"Pippo," called Peregrine a moment later.

Pippo grabbed up his cherry blossom and came through the gate.

"Come on," said Peregrine somewhat shortly.

Pippo fell into step beside him, yet with one anxious backward glance towards the ditch.

"The dog is out of pain," said Peregrine kindly. And Pippo drew a deep breath.

They still pursued their way in silence; at the moment words would not, I fancy, have come easily to either of them. Peregrine's face was still stern; Pippo's, if you must know, once more gleeful, something of a grin depicted on it. Since the victor had, it would appear, no vast satisfaction in the matter of the recent encounter, it behooved Pippo to have satisfaction for him, and this he had, very thoroughly.

Coming nearer the castle they found themselves by the church. The door was set wide open. It was hard upon the hour for Complin. Here Peregrine paused.

"Shall we enter?" he said, and passed through the porch.

Pippo followed him nothing loath, composing the muscles of his face into an expression better suited to the sacredness of the place. Since Peregrine had a mind to pray, pray he might. His own will in the matter might now be safely accorded him. In Pippo's eyes he had proved himself.

Pippo dropped on one knee before the hanging pyx, followed Peregrine into the dark oak pew. He saw the candles gleaming on the altar, their light commingling with the waning evening light. And over all was the quiet awe, the brooding stillness of the Hidden Presence.

A moment or so later a long line of monks entered the church, passed leisurely into the stalls.

"*Jube, domne, benedicere*," began the reader.

"*Noctem quietam, et finem perfectum concedat nobis Dominus omnipotens*," came the blessing.

Pippo glanced momentarily sideways at Peregrine's profile, saw his face peaceful, grave. A wave of sudden warmth struck on the boy's heart, a new admiration for the man beside him. He saw in him a fighting saint, a very St. George, protector of the weak and defenceless. Such another would he be himself in manhood, loving Christ and His Mother, champion of all wrong. The warmth at his heart brought a glow to his cheeks. The thought of his friendship raised him in his own estimation, which for that matter was at all times none so low. Anon he caught the sung words.

"*Irascimini, et nolite peccare....*"

To the context he paid little heed. Here again he saw Peregrine, saw him angered yet without sin, thrashing a very burly fellow soundly. Pippo, I fear me, paid but scant attention to the service; Peregrine absorbed his mind.

Later a movement brought him back to his surroundings. The monks were crossing to the statue of the Madonna, there to end the week with an antiphon in her honour. Somewhat tardily Pippo recognized his wandering thoughts.

"*Salve Regina, Mater misericordiæ*," he sang, his clear treble joining with the deeper voices, seeking to do atonement by the lustiness of his present singing. He gave full ear to the prayer that followed; crossed himself devoutly at the words, *Divinum auxilium maneat semper nobiscum*. Nevertheless his conscience pricked him somewhat.

The monks passed back into the sacristy. The candles on the altar were extinguished; the church was now in twilight, through which shone the soft red glow of the pyx-light.

Peregrine moved; and Pippo rose from his knees. Half way down the aisle he paused, slipped behind Peregrine, went back to the statue of Our Lady. At her feet he deposited his burden of cherry blossom, glanced up a moment half shyly at the tender face above him. Then turning swiftly he joined Peregrine without.

Peregrine, full of thought, had not noticed his absence. It was not till they were at the castle gates that he spoke.

"What hast thou done with the cherry blossom?" he demanded.

Pippo nodded his head backwards. "Oh, I left it down there," he replied airily enough. But he did not say that the snowy flowers lay before the Madonna as a small token of penitence for his wandering thoughts. Instead he spoke on a sudden in very different fashion.

"Feel my muscle," he said gravely, doubling back his arm.

CHAPTER VI

BALDA THE WITCH

THE days passed leisurely up at the castle, naught of vast import to mark their flight. June was now in, the month of roses, with long sunny days, with nights of brief duration.

Isabel, finding time hang somewhat heavy on her hands, turned yet closer attention to our Jester. Her interest in him had not waned; I am by no means sure that it had not increased. Recognizing his homage, she yet felt there was that in him which eluded her. Seeking to discover it she found herself baffled. While tantalizing it yet spurred her to further interest. Musing on the thought in her idle hours the desire to discover that which eluded her became somewhat of an obsession. She carried it with her throughout the day, took it to her couch as bedfellow.

Her women in these days found her ill to please. The dowager of them, one time in sort her nurse, now an old dame who seldom left her own chamber, never the castle, prescribed *tisanes* for her health, noxious concoctions of which the chief ingredient was the liquid from stewed rosemary, a mightily unpleasant herb to the palate. Mary would have her walk abroad, try fresh designs for her embroidery; and for my part I find her simple prescription wholesome. Leonora frankly saw mere ill-temper in her peevishness. Monica said rosaries for her, and truly prayer may take effect where all else fails. Brigid, very observant, said little, offered no remedies, but none the less she thought a good deal, fancied at one moment her thoughts were to some purpose, the next was none so sure of it. And then the clue came to her hand.

I know not how Isabel's mind began to turn upon the wise woman, so reputed, who dwelt in a mud-walled hovel in a distant combe among the moors. Perchance she happened at this time to catch some whisper of her from an over-credulous serving-wench; perchance the knowledge of the old crone's whereabouts had been with her before this, and now recurred fresh to her mind. Certain it is that Isabel, brooding, saw possibility of aid in that quarter. The notion was unquestionably prompted by foolishness, probably by something more evil. Once presented it conjoined with her former thought, not to leave. This, too, was a thought which might be brought to deed. Seeing this Isabel was ready to act. It was not her way to dally when she saw possibility before her.

One night sleep forsook Brigid's couch. Lying wide-eyed and wakeful an oppression fell upon her, not wholly of evil, yet something of that brand. Whispering an *Ave* she sought to free herself from it, yet to no purpose. *Paternosters*, the Sign of the Cross alike availed her naught. Moved by a sudden impulse she rose from her bed, went to the window.

Below her lay the garden bathed in quiet light. Beyond the shadow close beneath her window she could see clearly the expanse of turf, the gravel paths, the flower beds, all softly illumined in the moon-rays. Very still she watched, believing there was something about to happen, yet unknowing what it might be. At what exact moment a figure emerged from the shadow below her window Brigid knew not; suddenly she saw it, dark-robed, standing on the turf. For the space of a heart's beat the thought of some earth-bound spirit, some poor wandering ghost flashed to her mind, caused her a second's tremor. Yet a tremor succeeded verily by a greater shock. The figure turned, glanced momentarily towards the windows of the castle. Brigid saw the face clearly outlined in the moonlight, saw, too, in the movement one fearful of detection.

Swift as lightning she turned towards the room, threw garments upon herself with never a thought to their careful donning, slipped down the stairs and out into the soft June night. Here the garden lay silent, slumbering, no hint of restless figure to disturb its peace. Some might have believed themselves dreaming, illusioned, yet Brigid was very sure of her wakefulness, her sanity. Her mind brought quick to bear on possibilities she bethought her of the wicket gate beyond the lime trees, which led to the tiny copse fringing at that part the parkland. It would afford cover to one desirous of crossing the park unperceived by any watcher from the castle.

Brigid entered the copse. Here it was nearly dark, the moon-rays struggling fitfully through the thick-leaved branches overhead. Hastening, yet warily, fearful of coming too close upon the pursued and thereby discovering her pursuit, she made her way along the path, her ears alert to catch the sound of snapped twig ahead. Fearing imprudence she somewhat overdid her care, since, reaching the edge of the copse, she saw the figure far across the parkland, vanishing up the distant rise.

Brigid caught up her dress, sped forward hot-footed. Two thoughts were in her mind as she ran; one, that had she been closer on the scent there had been danger of the figure turning, and thereby detecting her in the open space of park, the trees being set wide apart; the other, that, should the pursued attain to the cross-roads up yonder before she once more gained sight of her, the scent would be truly lost, pursuit well-nigh hopeless, since of the end of this midnight roaming she had no inkling. This latter thought in mind she called the saints to her aid, and sped the faster. Though sound of wind and limb she was breathless as she breasted the top of the rise, had perforce to pause a moment's space; then she was on again, this time along a road. Turning a bend of it some hundred yards or so from the crossways, she saw the figure ahead of her, and thereupon put up a fervent thanksgiving. Slacking speed on the instant she crept cautiously along in the shadow of the hedge, keeping to the rough grass close below it, fearful lest the sound of her footfall should betray her pursuit.

At the cross-roads the figure turned to the left, Brigid following warily enough. The pace now giving time for reflection other than of mere pursuit, she fell to marvelling what this mad ramble portended. Had she not observed the half-scared glance towards the Castle she might have deemed Isabel sleep-walking, but having seen it this chance notion was dismissed with no second thought. There was purpose in this journey, and that a very definite one. But what purpose? Brigid cudgelled her brains to no end. A less clean mind than hers might have seen some dishonourable meeting ahead. Of such she had no thought. Frankly puzzled she found no solution of the riddle. Of what aid she might be in the matter afoot she thought not then any more than she had thought at the outset. Possibly at first curiosity had pricked her to the pursuit, though to my thinking it was chiefly some unconscious instinct of protection.

Presently the road divided, leftwards descending in a gentle decline, to the right branching in a rough track across the moorland. Isabel turned to the right. Dodging in the shadow of gorse bushes Brigid followed her. Verily must the matter on hand be of great moment. For no mere wild goose chase could Isabel be pursuing this desolate path at night. Dawning fatigue in a degree dulling interest Brigid began to experience some slight tremor at the loneliness to which she had come. The moorland stretched before her and on either hand, a vast undulating space broken by gorse bushes, distantly fringed by woods lying like dark patches in the moonlight. Once, far to the right, she caught a glimpse of moving antlers, where a herd of deer roamed among the heather. Awe at the silence and stillness clutched at her heart. Again she cried upon the saints. If you will believe me, Brigid gave them scant rest that night.

Topping a rise Isabel began to descend. Here the descent was steep, fell swiftly to a combe bottomed by a small copse. By the quickened pace of her Brigid believed she saw her journey's end in sight. Her own heart beat faster; fatigue in part forgotten, interest stirred anew.

At the bottom of the combe she saw a light, steady in the shadow under the hillside. Where there is a light there must needs be some creature to kindle the light; this was Brigid's judging. Yet who should dwell in that lonely place? And why, greater matter for surmise, should Isabel seek the dweller there? That she did seek him or her was very certain, since unfaltering she made her way towards the light. It came, Brigid now marked, from a mud hovel; the flame gleamed yellow through an aperture in the wall.

Isabel went up to the door, knocked. Brigid crouched breathless in the shadow of a bush. On the instant the flame was extinguished. The aperture sank back into the darkness of the wall. Brigid caught the murmur of Isabel's voice speaking. The door was opened cautiously. In the space she saw a woman's figure, bent, the head thrust forward. The moonlight falling on her face showed her of great age. The toothless mouth trembled and mumbled; the bleary eyes peered upwards from deep sockets; scant white locks fell across them. There came to her ear a further low murmur of words. Next Isabel entered the hovel; the door was shut.

Brigid sprang to her feet, the riddle well-nigh answered. Witchery of some sort Isabel had come to seek, white or black, it mattered little. White, it turned black in the fingering; black, it changed to very filth. Here she read the meaning of the oppression which had fallen upon her, which had held her wakeful.

"St. Brigid to her aid and mine," she whispered, making for the window, peering cautiously within. To make her presence known, to attempt persuasion in the matter, would be worse than fruitless; that she well knew. She had not served Isabel three years for nothing.

Her chin level with the window ledge, her eyes sought the interior of the hovel. In the dim glow of a peat fire she saw the room; a bare place enough, mud-floored, full of cobwebs and the thick scent of peat smoke. This scent and others more unwholesome caused a very vile odour. In one corner was a heap of heather and dried skins; across another, suspended by a frayed rope, hung a tattered curtain. A table, a bench, a chair on which sat Isabel, a stool for the hag, made up the furniture of the place.

The two were sitting by the hearth; Isabel upright, distaste very much in her bearing; the hag crouching towards the fire, holding claw-like hands to the warmth, muttering the while. Presently the muttering gave place to words.

"Greed, greed," came the mumbled speech. "Thou hast much; what more dost thou desire?"

"That which eludes me." The sound of the even, familiar voice in the vile-smelling place caused Brigid's heart to beat anew.

Balda the Witch laughed, a very mirthless sound, harsh as the scraping of iron on flint.

"Wait, then," she mumbled, straightening herself on the stool.

In the horrid silence Brigid stared towards the motionless figures, breath suspended. Her will beating back the horror that was creeping over her, she assured herself that this was foolishness in the guise of evil; yet the assurance brought her no vast solace. Further she told herself, being sane and healthy of mind, that it was the excitement of the midnight journey, the silence around her, which had wrought her nerves to a pitch of imagination, caused her to fancy darkness other than mere shadow lurking in the corners. Yet, for all that, she found herself whispering, "*Scuto circumdabit te veritas ejus: non timebis a timore nocturno.*"

For a space the silence endured, how long she knew not, having ceased to be aware of the passing moments. Then on a sudden came a sibilant murmur, seemingly from so great a distance that it was with fresh horror she realized it issued from one of the motionless figures by the hearth.

"That which thou dost desire is above thee. Yet must thou stoop to obtain it. Thus, and thus only canst thou grasp it, to wrest it from the Power where it lies." The voice stopped. A moment's silence followed on the words. Then once more came the voice, rising like a cry forced from an unwilling throat. "Yet who, with impunity, shall war with God? I, even I, Balda the Witch, say to thee, Beware."

Once more the silence fell. Brigid clutched the window ledge with shaking hands.

"This is all foolishness to the verge of madness," she whispered. A certain loyalty to Isabel, and, I fancy, terror lest the mere mention of her dread should draw it nearer, constrained her use of a harsher phrase.

Balda's figure relaxed from its rigid pose. Bending once more towards the fire she fell again to mumbling.

"Art frighted?" She stretched out one skinny claw, laid it on Isabel's wrist. "Good; I feel no tremor. Pride and desire should carry thee far along the road I have traversed. The hand is moist and cool. There is no fear here such as kneels quaking at the window." On the words she turned, pointing a palsied finger. Her red-rimmed eyes, deep in their sockets, looked straight at Brigid.

Had Brigid but known how nigh on empty of sight were those bleared terrible eyes, she had ducked below the window on the instant, made for the copse, and so escaped. Knowing it not, and seeing full accusation and discovery in the pointing finger, she knelt on, startled, turned to stone by the swiftness of the happening.

A moment at a loss for Balda's meaning Isabel still gazed at the fire, then realizing, she turned, saw the white wide-eyed face at the window.

"Brigid!" she cried, her voice on a harsh note of anger.

Isabel went straight to the door. Without she confronted Brigid risen from her knees. The two faced each other in the moonlight.

"Spy," said Isabel; that and no more.

Brigid, chin raised, uttered no word. She looked very straight at Isabel, who cared not to meet her eyes. There was certainly no shame in them.

Balda the Witch peered from the doorway. Well-nigh devoid of sight she scented the mental atmosphere, found that in the one woman ill-suited to her liking. Momentarily her spirit cowered. Muttering an oath she withdrew, slammed the door.

"Shall we return?" said Isabel silkily.

CHAPTER VII

SANCTUARY

THE Lady Abbess of Sangdieu, having heard vespers, was about to return to her own chamber, when word was brought her that one Mistress Brigid Carlisle was in the parlour seeking audience of her.

"My niece!" said the Abbess surprised, and startled for the moment from her customary equability of bearing.

"Even so, Reverend Mother," replied the nun. "She has ridden hence it would seem from some distance, attended but by a couple of serving men."

"Ah!" quoth the Abbess pondering. Then briefly, "Tell my niece I will be with her presently." Thereupon the nun withdrew.

A handsome old lady was this Abbess of Sangdieu; a rigid disciplinarian, stern, yet with no small strain of tenderness in her heart when you had found your way to it. Exceeding just, methinks she carried her sternness further towards herself than towards those over whom she had the rule. Of high rank, and very well-bred in courtesy that virtue extended itself throughout her domain; flowing naturally from the head it permeated those under her. Also, and this grace is by no means as common as some men would have us believe, she possessed humour. Descending to the parlour she found Brigid therein, white-faced and travel worn.

"Well, child," she said, giving her cheek to be kissed, "and what brings you here?"

"The desire for sanctuary," said Brigid very weary.

"Ha!" The old lady glanced sharply at her, read fatigue in every feature. Hospitality stirred quick within her. "First you must eat," she said. "Your story, for I see you have one, will keep. I will hear it anon."

Ringing a handbell, which was answered by a lay sister, she ordered food and wine to be brought. While waiting for its coming she put a question.

"How came you hither?"

"On horseback," replied Brigid. "The two men who rode with me are housing in the village. They will return at daybreak."

"Ah," mused the Lady Abbess. And a silence fell on the parlour.

A pleasant place it was, long and narrow, redolent of the cleanly smell of beeswax. The floor, very polished, bespoke good work with that material on the part of the lay sisters. Three windows looked on to the garden.

Roses climbing round them nodded crimson and yellow heads towards the room, their scent mingling with the smell of the beeswax. At one end was an open hearth, above which, on the wall, hung a white Figure on an ebony cross. A couple of pictures, some half-dozen chairs, and a deal table much scrubbed, made up the furniture. Bare enough truly, yet breathing an atmosphere of homeliness and peace. Brigid found in it a very haven of rest. Her tensioned nerves began to relax.

The lay sister appearing with a tray the Abbess roused herself to briskness. "Come, child, you must eat. Your face is as white as a kerchief. I would fain see a little colour in your cheeks."

While Brigid plied her knife and fork, she fell to studying her breviary, judging, and rightly, the girl would fare better deeming herself unwatched. Nevertheless her eyes were not wholly occupied with the book. What she saw in Brigid's face caused her some perplexity, though her manner gave no inkling of it. It was seldom the Lady Abbess's way to speak of what she saw; never on the instant. This gave time for seeing further, for weighing and for judging accurately. Thoughts surprised by another before they have come to full purpose have a way of taking sudden flight. Fearful of capture they fly on approach, and thereby good may be lost. The meal ended she laid the book aside.

"Now," she said, speaking cheerfully, "canst tell me thy story? Thy face is somewhat less like a washed-out dish-cloth."

"The Lady Isabel desires my services no longer," replied Brigid briefly.

"Indeed!" The Abbess's tone was somewhat grim. "And for what reason doth she no longer require them?"

"I have displeased her."

"Ah!" The old Abbess bent eagle eyes upon the girl. "And is her displeasure just?"

"I trow not," said Brigid very low.

"Tell me," said the Abbess briefly.

Brigid looked towards the windows. Through them, in the quiet garden, she saw two nuns walking. Beyond lay a yew hedge; beyond that again a low line of hills, blue against the sky. A thrush was singing in an elm tree.

"Tell me," repeated the Abbess.

"Madam, the story in its entirety is hers, not mine. I saw that which she desired not that I should see; I heard that which she desired not that I should hear. She was my mistress. For three years I received kindness at her hands. Therefore, for the telling, what I have said must suffice."

The Abbess nodded. Her mouth took on a line of grim approval. She liked loyalty.

"Good; it shall suffice. And now what do you propose?"

"To remain here." Brigid's voice was steady, though her face flushed.

"Ah! And in what capacity?"

"Madam, as nun."

The old Abbess looked up verily surprised. "Hoity toity, child; a nun is not made in a moment. 'Tis a question of vocation."

"I seek mine."

The Abbess pondered. "The desire is sudden."

"When God has a door to open methinks He can throw it wide on the moment an' He will. 'Tis every whit as simple to His power as a piecemeal opening."

The Abbess chuckled inwardly. She found in her niece's character something very akin to her own. Yet she replied gravely enough. "'Tis true; yet must we be sure 'tis God's Hand on the door and not our own."

"That," quoth Brigid very calmly, "may later be judged by you and the novice mistress."

Again the Abbess smiled, this time openly. "You go apace, child. We have not yet decided to accept you for your postulancy. True, from the world's standpoint, you have no permission to ask save mine, since your parents are dead,—God rest their souls. Well, well, we must see. My Lord Cardinal Falconieri proposes honouring the Minster with a visit some ten days hence. We will have his opinion on the matter. Till then certainly thou must bide here. Thou lookest as if the quiet of our house will stand thee in no ill stead." Then rising, "Come with me," she said. "I will take thee to thy chamber."

She led the way along cool passages, up wide oak stairs. Opening a door she entered a room facing west. The sun, not yet fully waning, poured through the window. It lay golden along the floor and on the white-washed walls. Brigid looked around her. Here was the same peace, the same homeliness she had found in the parlour below.

"You are very good to me, Madam," she said, her voice faintly a-tremble.

"Tut, child. Art thou not my own kin? Yet wert thou the veriest stranger I must needs give thee shelter, since thereby I might be entertaining an angel unawares. Not that I find thee exceeding like to one. I know thee and thy madcap ways over well for that mistake. Mind, child, no word of this thy purpose to any save myself. Now I will send Sister Bona to see that thou hast all necessaries. Haste thee to thy couch, child; thou art sadly weary. Christ have thee in His keeping." This time she offered not her own cheek for salute, but kissed the girl on the forehead. Then she left her.

On her departure Brigid crossed to the window, stood awhile looking out, yet with unseeing eyes.

CHAPTER VIII

COUNCIL AT SANGDIEU

HIS Eminence John Felix Maria Cardinal Falconieri having arrived at the Minster with such dignity of retinue as befitted a Prince of the Church, was closetted with the Lady Abbess.

A small, very old man this Lord Cardinal, at first sight you would have seen nothing remarkable in him. On first sight, I say, and that advisedly. Looking again, an' you were so minded, you would have guessed aristocracy in the thin-featured face, read kindliness in the mouth, shrewdness in the eyes, intellect in the forehead, and I am very sure determination in the chin. Had you received speech of him, you would have left mere surmise for certainty, and have added thereto a knowledge of his personality, his power.

Yet, for all that, you would have found him what he truly was, exceeding simple hearted. A stately progress, much retinue, irked him hugely. Yet he suffered the irksomeness on occasions, urged thereto by his chaplain, who recognized the dignity of his master vastly better than did the master himself; who held also that he knew very well what was good for both spiritual prince and subject. This prince's pleasure, and one he occasionally indulged in, was to escape in a manner temporarily from his rank in the Roman hierarchy, play *incognito* the part of simple priest.

There was a certain little church set on the edge of a forest, above a village containing some few hundred souls. Here at times he found the sheer simplicity he desired. Its priest dismissed to gain recreation an' he would in some wider sphere, the Cardinal took upon himself his duties. Here he said his daily Mass to the sound of the wind which whispered or shrilled through the forest trees according to the season, assoiled the souls of the village folk, gave them the Body of Christ to their refreshment; while never a breath of his true title got afloat. As Father Felix he was known among them; and, if you will believe me, they looked to his coming very willingly.

This little matter is not one which is set forth by his biographers. Had they got wind on it they would doubtless have fashioned a very pretty tale therefrom, garnished it out of all likeness of the simple truth. Hearing it not, however, it is omitted from their pages. You have, therefore, but my word for it.

Sitting now in a straight-backed arm-chair he thoughtfully surveyed an image of Our Lady on an oak bracket opposite to him, lending ear the while to the Abbess's discourse. A brief discourse truly. It was not her way to use two words where one sufficed, to elaborate unnecessarily. Clear-brained herself she looked for a like clarity in those with whom she conversed. Finding it frequently absent she prayed for patience. On this occasion no such prayer was needed.

Her discourse ended she fell to silence. Having said her say she left the verdict to other lips. An upright old figure, hands hidden in the sleeves of her gown, she sat waiting.

To another than the Abbess it might have appeared that her discourse had fallen on deaf ears, or at the least on ears for the moment closed to external sounds, since no reply followed on her words. You might have said, watching the Cardinal's face, that his wits had gone a-wool-gathering. Not so the Abbess. Perfectly serene she awaited the response she knew would come. Quiet reigned throughout the place; within the room entire, without broken only by an occasional footfall in the passage, by the faint jingle of beads as they swayed at the waist of some passing nun, or the liquid note of pigeons from the roof of the Minster.

Presently the Cardinal roused himself.

"Well, well," he said smiling, "send the child to me."

Brigid entering anon saw a small tired-looking old man sitting in a chair, his face towards the window. On her entrance he turned, and she saw no fatigue in the blue eyes. Kneeling she kissed his hand. He murmured words of blessing. Then—

"Be seated, child," he said.

He shifted his position, looked more directly at her.

"So thou hast left the Lady Isabel?"

"Aye, my Lord."

"And for what reason?"

"Sir, she desired my services no longer." Here was the same reply she had given to her aunt the Abbess.

The Cardinal put his hand up to his chin, looked at her very shrewdly.

"And perchance thou no longer desirest to serve her?" Here was a bow drawn at a venture, but the shaft shot very near the mark.

"My Lord—" stammered Brigid reddening.

"Suppose I hear the tale, my child."

"It is not wholly mine, my Lord."

The Cardinal smiled. "Well, we will leave it. The matter to my seeing stands thus. Thou hast displeased her, and thou art not wholly pleased with her."

"My Lord, I am very ill-pleased with her."

He laughed. "At least thou art candid, child. Now tell me truly, was there aught of pique in thy leaving the Castle."

"None, my Lord." The reply was ready enough. "I saw that she would not have me see, I heard that she would not have me hear. For that she liked me not, nor truly did I like her. I can no longer give her my service whole-heartedly, nor does she desire what lesser service I might give her. Therefore am I here." Again the reply she had given the Abbess, yet this time going further.

"Ah!" The fragile old hand beat lightly on the arm of the chair. "And here thou desirest to be a nun."

"That is my desire."

"A sudden desire, child."

"Sir," said Brigid very low and earnest, "may not Our Lord speak suddenly an' He will?"

"Very true," replied the Cardinal, "an' it be indeed His voice and not thy own heart speaking."

Brigid remained silent. The Cardinal bent kindly eyes towards her, read clearly resolve in the small square face. Musing, he shifted ground.

"Nuns pray much," he said warningly. "Thy aunt hath told me that on former occasions when thou hast visited the Minster prayer was none so greatly to thy liking."

"Mayhap, my Lord," said Brigid sweetly, "I can acquire liking. Here is a good school."

The Cardinal's eyes twinkled. Memory turning backward many years he saw the Lady Abbess herself before him, heard spoken words.

"Methinks, daughter," here was memory speaking, "thou lackest meekness, a quality possessed by nuns."

"Then, Father, it were well I seek it where it dwells so willingly."

Here he found a repetition of that little scene.

"I am also told, child," he continued, banishing memory for the moment, testing her replies, "that thou art over-merry. Nuns are sober-minded."

"Methinks, my Lord," quoth Brigid demurely, "that devotion on one note alone may prove a very monotonous chant."

Again the Cardinal's eyes twinkled. He liked the spirit that could find quick reply, fancied he saw here material other than usual for Sister Gabrielle the Novice Mistress, for all that saw her fashioning it willingly and to good purpose. Matters were not, however, wholly to his mind. Well-versed in dealing with mankind the girl's resolve was very patent to him. He would learn further what had brought the resolve to light.

"Child," he said on a sudden very grave, "thou hast told me little that is in thy mind."

Brigid looked towards the window. "My Lord," she said very low, "I lack words."

"Find those thou canst," he said kindly. "Perchance I may aid thee further."

Brigid trembled. "Sir, I have seen a soul in jeopardy."

"I have seen many, child. What then?"

"Ah, sir," said Brigid, her voice thrilling, "thinking on the one soul I thought on others. I saw a warring world, Powers in deadly conflict, Christ nailed to the Cross watching with Patient Eyes. Sir, I would aid."

"And how, child?"

"'Tis that I ask you, my Lord. Methought of ways and means, and found none. Then methought me of prayer. Sir, I am a woman, I can do but little. At the Foot of the Cross from whence Christ reigns can I not pray with Him in His Silence, in His Desire for the souls of men? My Lord, I have no words to show my meaning. Can you understand?"

The Cardinal looked not at her, but at the figure of the Mother of God. "I understand very well. Thou hast found words enough. And is that all?"

"All for which I can find the words, my Lord."

The Cardinal leaned back slowly in his chair. On the wall opposite him the sunlight lay in a brilliant patch creeping slowly upwards toward the blue-robed figure on the oak bracket. A silence endured a little space, a silence very pregnant with unuttered thoughts. Anon he roused himself, spoke almost briskly.

"Well, child, thou knowest Our Lord demands service in general from all souls, in particular from some. It would seem possible that He hath asked of thee an especial token of thy love towards Him. Whether it is precisely what those dost believe it to be cannot be decided on the instant. Yet for my part I see no hindrance—since thou hast no earthly ties to bind thee—to our putting the question to the test. Your part will be a very detailed obedience." He looked at her very kindly as she knelt to kiss his hand. On her departure he fell again into reverie.

Later he spoke to the Lady Abbess.

"Finding a certain likeness in the girl," quoth he with his shrewd old smile, "methinks we may fashion as very excellent a nun from the niece as the aunt hath proved herself."

"Truly, my Lord," retorted the old lady, "with my aid to the balance in the matter I trust you will fashion a better one."

CHAPTER IX

THE CASTING OF THE NET

LOYALTY holding Brigid silent concerning certain matters between her and the Lady Isabel, we, owing none, may well probe somewhat further, though doubtless the manner of the happening is already patent to you.

Isabel had found discovery exceeding unpleasant to her mind. A hidden good disclosed may irk men somewhat, a hidden evil disclosed will irk them very surely. Isabel brooked it not at all. Anger possessed her soul. Hereafter she would ever see reproach in the girl's eyes, read condemnation in her very silence. So unpleasant a state of things was assuredly not to be suffered. Nor was it discovery alone that displeased her. Conscience pricking tardily showed her that night's work as very ill. Compunction in a manner was present with her, yet no true sorrow. Desirous of forgetting it she was willing to profit by what knowledge it had brought her. Yet forgetfulness were impossible with Brigid's eyes to remind her of it.

Her spirit rebelled at the thought. She would have all men see in her the perfection she desired them to perceive. An' she could not lull Brigid's mind to a like forgetfulness, wake once more in her the full homage she believed ever to have received of her, she desired her presence no longer. There was the matter very plainly. It lay wholly between her and the girl. The warfare—for such after a manner it became—had place in private. It was of brief duration. To outward seeming Isabel was the victor, yet to my thinking it was Brigid who had triumphed, since never for an instant had Isabel's will gained the mastery over hers.

A faint whisper of evil, very subtly set afloat, caused the court to look askance at her. Some few cried, "I cannot believe it," yet rather in false piety than as true statement of disbelief. Certainly the evil remained unproven, since none sought to prove it, caring little in the matter. As for Brigid, the whisper was too faint to gain her ears. Later it grew somewhat louder, when she was beyond its reach. Then it was left to Mary Chester to defend her, which she did right royally.

In the small hours of the morning Brigid rode away, the sun not far above the horizon, the dew yet heavy on the grass. Pippo, his arms full of flowers he had culled for her from the garden, was at the postern gate to watch her depart.

"God keep you," he said as she took his flower burden from him. Peregrine using the salutation at times he now used it himself, though shyly.

"God keep you too, Pippo," she said, smiling her thanks for his gift.

Anon, turning in her saddle, she waved her hand to him. Mary Chester's friendship, and Pippo's bright face were her pleasantest memories of the life she was leaving. Here, too, were the child's flowers in her arms. Thus she rode away to Sangdieu, as we have seen.

Isabel rejoiced at her departure, felt herself free for the matter she had in hand. Throwing aside all thought of a certain night that June, she yet retained in part the memory of the words then given her.

"That which thou dost desire is above thee. Yet must thou stoop to attain it."

On the further speech she did not care to dwell. This utterance sufficed her. Quick-witted, she saw very clearly the significance therein. It behooved her merely to act upon it. Here was a delicate matter, requiring careful handling. She had no mind to see herself caught in the meshes she would spread for another, a thing just possible to her shrewd thinking. She must throw the light cords deftly, that no breath of fancy should recoil them on herself. This, for all the seeming poetry of the task, would require an exceeding level head, a cool and very calculating judgment.

With care she conned the part she saw herself about to play, marked her entrance with the meshes, made very sure of her exits. Having it to her mind at her finger tips she waited for Chance to set the stage.

To leave matters to Chance is at times to leave matters half way to the Devil. An' he is so minded he will come the other half to meet them. Verily to my thinking he did so now, took them in hand and arranged them with age-old skill, exceeding simply. And to this purpose he used a garden for his first setting.

Isabel walking in the garden one morning of soft air and sunshine saw Peregrine by the sundial. A favourite position this for our Jester.

Seating herself on the stone balustrade of the terrace she raised her hand, beckoned him to her. He came, stood before her, his eyes alight like a child's who has been called by a close friend.

"I am weary," she said softly.

"Truly, Madam!" quoth Peregrine very astonished. Here was no day for weariness. Sun-kissed, splendid in light and colour, the earth breathed vitality and joy.

"Of my own company," said Isabel, smiling at his look.

"Madam," stammered Peregrine, "I will fetch your women to you."

She laughed outright very musically. "That is like to a man," she said. "An' they were here I were none the less weary." She fetched a little sigh.

"Madam," said Peregrine troubled.

She looked across the moorland, sadness in her eyes. "Aye," she said on a faint note of bitterness, "soul-weary."

"Madam," said Peregrine for the third time, any word but the one hard to find.

"Methinks," she said very low, "that the loneliness of a woman seemingly surrounded by many friends is a very bitter loneliness. She looks for understanding and finds it not. Those she has counted as truest to her may ofttimes play her false, revile her, and leave her. Yet to revile in turn were ill done. She must smile when her heart is sore; laugh when her spirit is bruised and bleeding, lest she bring sadness into other lives." She stopped.

"Madam," said Peregrine very earnestly, anger towards Brigid in his soul, "there is at least one heart would suffer death gladly for your sake."

"Ah," she smiled sadly, "at times I have dreamed so. Yet where can I put trust? They offer me homage with their lips yet none with their hearts. Outwardly they speak me fair, inwardly they see me shallow. Do you think me shallow, Peregrine?" Here was a note of pleading as from a child.

"Never," said Peregrine hotly.

She looked at him very strangely. "An' you speak so with your heart in your voice it tempts me to believe you. You are Jester, Peregrine; yet methinks the fool's motley but hides the heart of a loyal man. Is it so, Peregrine?" She lingered on the name.

"Madam," said Peregrine, the heart in question beating very hotly, "it beats in your service alone."

"You, too, are lonely?"

"Madam, it was so at one time."

"And now?"

"Since you have shown me favour, since you have deigned to see the man beneath the motley, my heart has been too full for loneliness."

"I think," she said softly, musing, "we understand each other very well. It is strange, is it not, it should be so? I, Isabel de Belisle, and you a Jester, the meanest of my household, so men would say, and we hold a bond of understanding between us. Let us not heed what men would say. I have told you they see me very shallow. 'Tis sweet to me to think you believe it not. Shall we keep our understanding a secret between us," she held out her hand.

Dropping on one knee he kissed it very humbly. Had she demanded his soul from him at that instant he had given it, believing it were better in her keeping than in his own. Perchance she had spoken again, but Mary Chester came softly across the grass, saw the two with eyes faintly troubled.

Hereafter there were days of sweet glamour for Peregrine. That he was understood he had guessed before in part, as we have seen. Here now were the words from his lady's very lips. Of all those who did her service none knew her as he knew her, none saw the depths beneath the sparkling surface, none saw the heart-loneliness beneath the radiant smile.

Days followed on days, outwardly the same, yet holding many an exchange of glances, many a tender half-uttered sigh, now and again an unwatched meeting. There were hours in her chamber when he sang to her among her women, each word holding a meaning known to the two alone; hours in the garden in the full radiance of sun and colour, when every bird that sang, when every flower that bloomed poured benediction on them; and—quintessence of joy—rare solitary meetings, when heart spoke freely to heart in low tender words. Small wonder he forgot all else in the thought of her. Even Pippo's artless companionship became at times burdensome to him.

So she lured him on, saw the white flame of his adoration turn to red with the fuel of her giving. And softly day by day she threw closer meshes round his soul. Unsuspecting, it struggled not at all, made no attempt to escape.

Isabel smiled. The Devil, who had set the stage, I am very sure laughed. At Sangdieu Brigid prayed.

CHAPTER X

WITHERED ROSES

FOOL You cry in your heart, and perchance again, Fool! Yet for my part I find his folly in a manner to my liking. I had liefer see a man prodigal of his gifts, though he bestow them on an unworthy object, than see him a niggard, grudging in his giving.

But, an' you would know him truly, he saw not himself as giving, believed not that he bestowed gifts, believed himself merely the recipient of them. Wherein the wrong lay verily was that he forgot the Creator in the created. This you will have doubtless guessed already; it needs not that I show it you.

An' you call to mind the prophecy of the old sage, who read the message of the stars at his birth, you will remember his foretelling; see Peregrine here the recipient of favours from one of high birth, will look to their withering like June roses when picked. Now to the manner of their withering.

It will be found in the chronicles of the Lords of Belisle that in a certain year of Grace, on the Feast of St. Mary Magdalene, one Count Bonaventure de Novello came to the Castle, bearing letters from Lord Robert to his daughter Isabel. It is further shown that he was received with hospitality, and remained for a time as a favoured guest of the Castle. The manner of his departure is not so clearly given, but one may guess that he departed in somewhat lesser favour. Yet it is neither his departure nor the manner of it that concerns us chiefly, but rather his arrival and his sojourn.

A comely man this Bonaventure de Novello, so I have heard; of average height, olive-skinned, and bright-eyed. He could dance, he could sing; he had moreover a very pretty wit, and a tongue that knew well the handling of it. Up to a point it stood him in better stead than rapier, since the tongue may madden more readily than steel; the point passed the rapier was not lacking in its skill. In the matter of love he made it not at all, since he got plenty without his making, and scorned it accordingly. It was the same, I take it, with homage, liking, or any other favour. Therefore you will see Isabel looking queerly on him at the first, since it was ever her way to receive willingly rather than to give. Anon she began to exercise her customary wiles over him. Finding him none too easy to lure the task absorbed her. We may see Peregrine forgotten. Here it was that his roses began to wither.

It is no easy task to show you Peregrine at this time. Very silent, showing his mind to none, one can but guess at it. I fancy he saw at first in Isabel's bearing but the natural extra courtesy to a new-comer, a guest. Found—before a stranger—her apparent indifference towards himself to be expected. For a time he suffered it gladly, seeing himself thereby enduring a trifle of hardship for her sake, and at her will. Anon perplexity dawned upon his soul. A dog look crept into his eyes, the wonder of a dumb animal who believes he has displeased, yet knows not the manner of the displeasing; who holds none the less utter faith in his master. A word, a look at this time would have restored full buoyancy to his heart. None came, therefore he suffered mutely.

"Truly you possess a very merry Jester," quoth the Count one day, light sarcasm in the words.

"A dull fellow," said Isabel idly.

"He eyes you like a dog at one time fondled, now relegated to the courtyard," laughed Bonaventure. Easily uttered, spoken wholly in jest, the words shot very straight to Isabel's heart, dyed her face with faint colour.

"An' his sire had not been Jester before him, I would have none of him," she answered a thought over-readily. "Custom gave him the cap and bells which he wears, as you perceive, with a very long face."

Bonaventure laughed again. "An' but custom gave him the motley, methinks I would override custom," he responded. And thereupon turned to other matters.

His words, however, remained with Isabel. Plainly, she was weary of the Jester. Body and soul she saw him hers; there was no longer aught to gain. Also she misliked very heartily the dumb pleading of his eyes. Weariness turned to impatience, impatience to something akin to anger. What right had he to stir compunction in her? Her favours were her own to give or withhold at will. Given, they must be received with gratitude; withheld, there must be no whining. Yet Peregrine had never whined; he had, however, looked with the eyes of a dumb dog.

Sitting in her chamber she brooded somewhat sullenly on the matter. After some space a thought came to her, gradually crystallizing. Bonaventure might perchance aid her in dealing with the affair. Here she calculated briefly, lightly. It would entail a slight wandering from the truth. What then? Truth it happened was of less consideration to her than ease of mind. From the one thought she turned to others. They followed each other quickly. Purposing to wrong the Jester, hatred followed swiftly in its train. There is ever but a step between the two. Her revolution of feeling towards him being sudden was proportionately strong. It brought ice to her heart, not heat. This is the more dangerous, since with it there is no surcharging of the brain to unbalance thought. Briefly, she would say to Bonaventure, "Rid me of this man," yet employ not those words at all. Her request simply put in other fashion it would remain to see if he accepted it with a like simplicity, if a dealing that smacks very surely of meanness may be termed simple.

Being alone with the Count she spoke to him very levelly.

"A while ago you mentioned our long-faced Jester."

"Truly, Madam, I did," replied Bonaventure, "yet have small desire to mention him again. I had as lief dwell on an east wind blight."

Isabel smiled, then sighed. "An' my father had not given him the post I would have none of him. In his absence I like not to oust his servants." A very dutiful daughter, she sighed more deeply.

"You would an' you could?" he queried.

"He hath done no ill," said Isabel musing. "'Tis wrong of me thus to mislike him, and foolish truly, since why should I concern myself with the fellow at all? Yet 'tis, as you say, the east wind blight that causes me to shiver."

Bonaventure smiled. Truly the transparency of her desire was very patent. An' he would he saw himself giving aid in the matter. Considering a brief space he decided to take it in hand, this rather from light mischief than any ill-will towards Peregrine.

"Truly, as you say," said he solemn-faced, "the fellow has done no ill. 'Twere unjust to hold him to account for a long visage and a hang-dog look. He is also a peaceable man."

"Very peaceable," averred Isabel.

"Then 'tis evident he must bide here, since 'tis your father's pleasure." He looked not at Isabel as he spoke; but she, glancing side-ways at his face, was by no means so ill-satisfied at what she saw there. Matters to her mind were put in train.

Feeling them so, pity brought a slight thaw to hatred. Once she smiled on the Jester, gave her hand to be kissed on the conclusion of a song that pleased her. Light tokens truly, yet hope springing swift anew to Peregrine's heart the subsequent happenings were the more bitter.

One morning Isabel sitting in her chamber heard voices below her window. The words themselves reached her not, yet the tone was apparent to her. There was the Count's smooth, exceeding silky; Peregrine's holding exasperation for the moment well controlled.

Seemingly unheeding she yet listened intently. Mary Chester raised anxious eyes from her embroidery; Leonora calm as her mistress, worked steadily; Monica, paling, fingered her rosary.

Anon the Count laughed. Light though the sound was it held a stinging note. Peregrine's voice rose somewhat harder.

"Madam," breathed Mary very low some unnamed fear clutching at her heart.

Isabel looked towards her. "Yes?" she queried, eyebrows raised.

"'Tis naught," stammered Mary reddening, words halting on her tongue.

"Ah!" The exclamation came from without. Though holding pain, Mary detected triumph in the sound. She moved very swiftly to the window.

"Madam!" she said again in horror.

"What is it?" asked Isabel quickly.

"The Count Bonaventure lies upon the ground," stammered Mary. "Methinks that Peregrine—" she broke off trembling.

Isabel joined her at the window.

"Go below, see to what hath chanced," she ordered. And to herself she added, "I pray Count Bonaventure hath not over-reached himself in the matter."

Ill news flies very swiftly. Within the space of five minutes the whole Castle was agog with the happening. Peregrine the Jester had stabbed Count Bonaventure. True the wound was not over-serious, yet that was rather by good fortune than by good intention. Some half hour later Peregrine lay in the cellar; the Count, his wound bound, made light of the matter.

"I can take it none so easily," said Isabel hard-eyed.

"The fellow should be hanged," said Roger March, the captain of the guard, very bluntly. These were rude times, and Roger a hard-headed soldier.

"Bah!" laughed Bonaventure ruefully, "'tis no matter for so harsh dealing." Already he half-regretted his part in the affair. He liked Peregrine for his onslaught; saw the tongue a mean weapon to have used for his provoking.

Isabel's eyes narrowed. "I cannot overlook it," she repeated very cold, seeing opportunity slipping from her.

"Shall he hang, Madam?" asked Roger briefly.

"By the Lord, no," burst forth the Count. "You will not have a woman give orders to hang a man. An' he deserve punishment give him a drubbing and dismiss him the Castle. So shall all be satisfied," he added half maliciously.

Roger looked at Isabel, awaited her pleasure.

"You have heard the Count's words," said Isabel very icily. "The injured may assign his own reward for the injury. I leave the affair."

Roger March saluted and withdrew.

The Count, by the window, drummed lightly on the sill with his fingers, looked not at Isabel standing rigid by the hearth. The mental atmosphere held an unpleasant chill.

Sudden sounds broke the silence; trampling of feet on the stairway, exclamations of anger.

Isabel and the Count faced about towards the door. The heavy draperies of the curtain swung aside. Peregrine burst into the room, fell on his knees before Isabel.

"Madam," he cried thickly, imploring, "I come to crave pardon. Allot me what punishment you will, but dismiss me not from your presence." The words were out of his lips ere the captain of the guard and two of his men had gained the chamber. Beyond the swaying curtain was a group of women with scared faces.

The Count looked at the kneeling figure; the somewhat cynical smile on his lips was not for it. From the Jester he glanced at Isabel.

"Take the fellow away," said Isabel.

At the sound of her voice Peregrine looked up at her face. Realization dawned on him. He got to his feet, staggering like a man dazed with over-much wine.

"Your will, Madam?" said Roger sternly. He trusted now to find his hands busy with the rope.

"I have given you my orders already," said Isabel harshly.

Roger March, grim-faced, led Peregrine away.

The Count looked at Isabel. Meeting her eyes very full he smiled mockingly.

CHAPTER XI

OUTCASTE

THUS a second time we see Peregrine dismissed the Castle.

Exceeding sore in body, yet infinitely more sore in mind, he lay in a wood some two miles or so from the spot where the last blow had fallen upon him. Half fainting he had dragged himself thither. Roger March had been in no mind to see light punishment dealt out.

For a time a sort of stupor fell on him, dulling in part the pain of body and soul. A sick man half delirious he felt himself, tortured by very evil dreams. Mocking faces surrounded him, and in their midst one face very cold, looking at him with eyes full of scorn and hatred. Then, for a while, the lapse of years escaping him, he believed himself a child burying a hot face in his mother's gown, weeping out his woes in her lap. Later he found the lap to be that of Mother Earth, her gown the cool green of the moss against his cheek. Turning his head he saw the green-leaved branches above him, had a glimpse of summer blue sky. This brought him back to the present. He sat up feeling the swelled stiffness of his back and limbs.

Some hundred yards or so before him his eye caught the glint of water among the trees. He remembered that he was very thirsty. He rose stiffly to his feet, made his way towards the pond. It lay clear as a mirror, reflecting the trees.

Peregrine, kneeling at the margin, bent towards it, saw a haggard-faced Jester looking up at him. For a moment startled by his own reflection he drew back; then laughed. Hard-eyed he looked at his own image; on a sudden saw himself Jester to Fate. Here was his rôle with a vengeance. He looked at his own face again, and with new interest, grinned at it a moment very diabolically. The next, he dashed his fist in the water. The reflection shivered to a thousand sparkling fragments.

"To Fate's Jester," he cried. And he drank thirstily from his cupped hand.

A crackling in the woods behind him brought him to his feet. His frayed nerves tensioned he gazed towards the bushes. From among them came a small figure in blue and silver, glancing anxious-eyed to right and left. Seeing Peregrine the boy rushed forward, flung himself before him, clasped his knees.

"Peregrine, Peregrine," he sobbed. "Oh! the brutes. Would I were a man!"

Peregrine hauled the child gently to his feet.

"Tut, lad," he said lightly, "'tis all in the day's work."

The boy snivelled in his sleeve. His cheeks were very tear-glazed.

"An' thou wert the man thou desirest to be thou wouldst not weep," said Peregrine seating himself on the ground, drawing the child beside him.

"My heart would," choked the boy.

Peregrine finding grim truth in the reply made no answer.

"I hate them all," said Pippo, his young face very vicious. At that Peregrine laughed mirthlessly.

"I will not return to the Castle," said the boy stubbornly, "I will come with you."

Peregrine fell grave on the instant. He saw not a child travelling by the road he was like to follow.

"Nay," he responded firmly.

"I must," choked Pippo.

"Thou wilt return to the Castle," said Peregrine very levelly.

"Why?" demanded Pippo.

Peregrine smiled. "Firstly, not being my property I cannot carry thee away with me; secondly, my road is not like to be one for a child; thirdly, I wish thee to return, Pippo."

Pippo's mouth trembled. "For thirdly I will do your bidding," he said in a very small voice. "I would not for firstly nor secondly."

"Good lad," said Peregrine.

For some moments there was silence. Pippo's face was quivering; Peregrine's very set and stern.

"So, boy, it is farewell," he quoth anon. Pippo found his voice too shaky for speech.

Peregrine got to his feet, the lad with him. "I will take thee to the edge of the wood," he said.

In silence they made their way among the trees. In some ten minutes they found themselves on their outskirts. Here Peregrine paused.

"Farewell, lad," he said. "Put not your trust in princes, as the Psalmist hath it. Pray to Christ and Our Lady, and live clean." Smiling grimly at the words himself he had to give them to the lad. A child's faith must be left unshaken. Peregrine having this thought in mind doubtless the Recording Angel made tally of the speech to his balance.

He kissed the boy twice, and without more ado turned back among the trees, mistrusting himself for further words. Pippo went sorrowfully enough down the hill.

Peregrine struck again clean through the wood. The Castle thus lay behind him, and the greater distance he might put between himself and it the better now would he be pleased.

He made his way along the soft path, cool green for the most part, here and there scattered with dancing spots of gold as the sunlight filtered through the branches overhead. On either hand were tree trunks, straight as the pillars of some cathedral, flecked with the orange and silver of fungus and lichen, very brilliant patches of colour. It was a silent place, quiet and restful. Formerly Peregrine's spirit had gone out to meet the spirit of the woods, to find pleasure in the meeting. Now he found none. Disillusionment pressing sore upon him crushed his soul very bitterly.

At last, after some time of walking, he came upon the edge of the wood. Here it was bordered by the high road, very white and dusty, the sun's rays beating full upon it. To the right it ascended somewhat, to the left it sloped in a gentle decline. Peregrine hesitated. He had no goal in view, nor sought to have any.

While hesitating he became aware of a party of three horsemen riding at a trot from the leftwards. He drew into the shadow of the trees to await their passing. Coming abreast of them he saw in the foremost the Count Bonaventure, the other two being serving men. The Count wore his left arm in a sling, a matter that Peregrine marked with no little satisfaction. Allowing them to pass some couple of hundred yards or so, he stepped from the wood, turned down the hill. He had made but a few paces when the sound of a horse's hoofs behind him struck on his ear. He stepped quickly towards the hedge. The horse and its rider pulled up along side of him.

"I saw you among the trees," said Bonaventure without preamble.

"What then?" demanded Peregrine, the pupils of his eyes narrowing.

"Merely," quoth the Count lightly, "that I wish to make you an apology."

"No need," said Peregrine shortly.

"Yet I did you an injury."

"Methinks I did you one," said Peregrine, looking at the bound arm.

"'Tis one will mend," was the reply.

Peregrine was silent.

"Yet, perchance," said the Count musing, "the injury I did you was not so great as at first sight might appear."

"I find it a benefit," said Peregrine very dryly.

"Ha!"

"An' a man pitch his tent on a vile bog believing it fair earth 'twere a benefit to drag him from it, even though the handling be somewhat rough."

"Oh!" said the Count amazed, opening his eyes wide, "you have seen that."

"I have seen more than that," said Peregrine.

"Yes?" queried the Count.

"I have seen that you," said Peregrine watching him, "acted as subtly prompted, if not fairly told."

The Count stroked his chin, half whimsical, half vexed. He was not wholly pleased to be named a tool in the matter, which he truly was.

"I think you have seen a good deal," quoth he ruefully.

"Disillusionment clears a man's eyesight," said Peregrine shortly.

"Humph!" remarked the Count. "Where fare you now?" he demanded.

Peregrine shrugged his shoulders. "Where Chance leads. Mayhap to the Devil."

"An unpleasant fellow," said the Count suavely, "and moreover no gentleman."

"Truly!"

"A very usurer. Getting a man in his debt he demands constant interest, exceeding extortionate."

"An' a man were wise he would return the whole loan and have done with the matter," returned Peregrine carelessly.

"No man has sufficient capital for that when he once takes loan from the Devil," replied the Count half grimly.

"You seem to have a very good knowledge of his dealings," said Peregrine.

Bonaventure shrugged his shoulders. "I have observed them more than once," he said coolly. "An' you have no better prospect in view than perchance to serve him, will you join company with me?"

Peregrine shook his head. "No," he said.

"I am barely surprised," returned the Count. "Yet I would ask you, unaccountable as it may seem to you, to come as my friend, not as my servant."

Peregrine laughed. "I put no trust in friends."

"That also does not surprise me," said Bonaventure. "I put not vast trust neither, but take men as I find them."

"Then you will not find much," retorted Peregrine.

"I do not look for much."

"That shows you wise."

Bonaventure laughed. "Wisdom is what I seek. Perchance some day I shall find her. However since you will not seek her in my company I must e'en bid you farewell."

"Farewell," said Peregrine.

"We part on good terms?"

"In no enmity as far as I am concerned," said Peregrine carelessly.

"Then again, farewell," quoth the Count. Turning his horse he rode quickly after his men. Peregrine stood looking after him.

CHAPTER XII

THE WANDERER

WITHIN a certain forest was a Castle, hidden tolerably deep within it. It lay not many miles from the Castle of Belisle, which stood upon an eminence. Though hidden from it by the surrounding trees the dwellers at Belisle knew of its existence. It was named, so I have heard, Castle Syrtes. It had a somewhat unwholesome reputation; it has also been termed magical in an evil manner.

You came upon it by tortuous paths through the forest, the outskirts of which were slushy and boggy to the feet. Having passed the outskirts you could find paths in plenty. Despite their tortuous winding they led eventually to the Castle. Outwardly pleasing to the eye, built of a reddish stone brought from no man knew where, the interior pleased the senses no less. Here were marble halls, shaded bowers, silken curtains, pictures very subtly painted, rare curios brought from home and lands beyond the seas. Flowers within and without, many-coloured and full-perfumed, lent a sweet and somewhat heavy scent to the atmosphere. It was never wind-lifted. The winds, which at times blew freely on the outskirts of the forest, brought no cleansing breath to the interior. Perchance the trees grew too thickly to allow of it passing between their branches; perchance there was some deeper reason. For that you may make what judgment you choose. My part is to set forth facts as I know them.

Within the Castle dwelt a woman named Thaïs. To my thinking she had been better named Venus or Aphrodite. Failing either of those names Thaïs suits her not ill-well. She did not dwell alone; solitude would have been by no means to her liking. Guests she had in plenty, and they fared very luxuriously at her hands. The days were passed in feasting and pleasure; song, music, and wine lent good aid thereto. In brief the existence was one of exceeding soft luxury.

At times a guest wearied of the pastimes, found them over sweet to his taste. Such a one was known now and again to leave the Castle; but I have heard it given as fact, which fact may be noteworthy, that he found the return through the forest more wearisome than the approach. Thorns and brambles, which stood aside to let him pass on entrance, hedged his path sadly on departure. Perchance herein lay its reputation for evil-magic. Certain it is the forest was strange, very dark, and full of a sweet sickly odour. No fresh-scented flowers grew there, such as one may find in open meadows and cool breeze-swept woods, but curious orchids, spotted and twisted, reptile-like in colour and form. Also no song-birds penetrated to its depths, misliking the darkness.

What brought Peregrine thither I know not, seeing he had at the first wandered many a day's march from Belisle. Possibly he circled thereto unheeding his route, knowing not he was returning on his own traces.

Be that as it may, one evening at sundown he saw the forest facing him. It lay a dark patch on the horizon, backed by torn clouds through which the sunset sky showed red and lurid. Around him was the pathless earth, rough and very desolate. No sign of human habitation was in sight. Rocky boulders flung up here and there among the coarse-grassed earth loomed with uncouth shapes in the waning light. To his thinking they seemed cast there by some mighty spirit in grim play; one, who, wearying of the game, had withdrawn to some distant region, the loneliness now emphasized by his one-time presence there.

Behind the forest the torn clouds began piecing together in a heaped ominous mass, the red light obliterated. The heavy air, exceeding sultry, bespoke storm. Far off, to the right, he saw a white road climbing a hillside. A bare tree, set where the top of the hill touched the sky, flung a couple of branches wide-spread from its trunk. Cross-like it crowned the summit; leafless, dead, yet symbol of the Tree of Life.

Peregrine looked towards the road. Doubtless it led some whither. But where? There was the question. Also it was far off and very steep. A storm was brewing. Already he could hear the low muttering of thunder. To gain yonder road and seek some distant shelter along it would entail a very thorough drenching before any goal had been attained. The forest was but a quarter the distance from him. He might well seek harbourage there.

Yet, despite the thought, his eyes turned again towards the distant road. An' he were sure of shelter beyond the summit of the climb he might risk the storm which very certainly would break upon him. For the space of some moments he hesitated. Then common sense won the day. The white road might lead him but on some fool's errand. Before him lay obvious cover from the oncoming deluge. He stepped out across the coarse grass, now hastening his steps somewhat. Nearing the forest the grass became shorter and smoother, but here the bog began to show itself.

"I bargained not for this," said Peregrine, as his feet sank into the slush. Even as he spoke heavy drops began to fall; thunder muttered very ominously. A third time he glanced towards the distant road.

"Bah!" he said, "'tis too far off. A sharp transit, and shelter will be gained." He made quick strides forward. The atmosphere, which had been windless, was suddenly rent by a heavy blast. "Now it comes," said

Peregrine, as the storm beat upon him, and the rain sluiced down on the sodden earth.

"A very miry way," muttered Peregrine breathless as he gained the margin of the forest, looked ruefully down at his feet. Turning, he looked behind him. Where had been spongey earth were now wide pools, stung by falling rain, whipped by slashing wind. The further landscape was blotted out by mist and quick-gathering dusk.

"A most villainous storm," said Peregrine, "and it is well I have found cover from it. Here I must bide for a while at least. There is no re-crossing that morass."

Now he must think what to do. To sit quiet where he was, and watch the rain were dull and dismal work. For all that the forest was very dark it might be well to explore somewhat further. He turned down a winding path. In spite of the first sense of darkness he was now aware of a curious light glimmering through the place. This came, he saw, from some strange fungus on the trunks of the trees, which gave forth an uncanny illumination. It was faint truly, but sufficed to show the path before him.

As he walked, the odour of the forest struck upon his nostrils, heavy, sickly-sweet. Passing to his brain it dulled his senses somewhat, like the odour of a powerful drug. He found himself pursuing his way after the manner of a man half-dreaming, heedless now of where his path might lead. Half drowsed though he was he noted now and again the orchids that grew among the trees, saw their spotted hue, their twisted reptile-like form. Despite his drowsiness he felt some slight repulsion at the sight of them, thought momentarily on sun-kissed flowers in open meadows. By contrast the orchids fared ill in his mind. But sleep clutching at his eyelids made thought an effort.

He stumbled onward very heavily. How long he walked he knew not. It might have been an hour, two hours; yet, time perchance being as leaden-footed as he, it might have been a bare ten minutes.

Suddenly, with no volition on his own part, his brain swung from dulness, roused itself to action; and strange action truly. It awakened, it would seem, from stupor to fantastic delirium. He felt himself vividly alive, and utterly alone. Alone he was verily in that forest devoid of living creatures. Yet the loneliness was of spirit rather than of body. In that moment his spirit was caught up into space. Knowing the earth beneath him, solid, material, around and above him were vast distances, deep silences. In the furthest distance, in the deepest silence, at so great an altitude that his brain seeing it reeled, gleamed a great star. Now here was the fuller fantasy. Within the depth of his own soul he was conscious of a like spot of light, a glowing star, yet very tiny. And he knew that between the star within him and the star above him was a strange attraction.

In space then his spirit hung, poised on nothingness, so it seemed. And here he was aware that he himself held his soul thus poised. By will he could clutch at the earth beneath him, draw himself down to it; by relinquishment of will he could be drawn, by virtue of the star within him, into the distance to the other star, infinitely remote. Deep silence lay around him, a hush as of expectation and waiting. To him like a breath of wind from far-off places came the words, *"Excelsus super omnes gentes Dominus, et super cælus gloria ejus."* He knew now what it meant; saw in a lightning flash where the choice lay. Yet the vastness above him filled him with terror. A strange cowardice seized upon him; a frantic desire for the material, the solid. Madly his will clutched at the earth beneath him....

He found himself walking in the forest, the stupor and the delirium alike passed. And now he was very sure he had been dreaming. Once more his brain was clear and steady. He half mocked at himself for his brief delusion.

Some half-dozen paces further on the trees thinned on a sudden. He came out upon a smooth grass sward beyond which stood a Castle, the light streaming from the windows.

CHAPTER XIII

CASTLE SYRTES

TRULY I would have thought, and you would have thought, and we might well imagine Peregrine would have thought, he had had enough of castles and the dwellers therein. Yet there is no question but that he welcomed very heartily its appearance before him. Here at least was the tangible, the solid, the very definitely material to counteract the sudden and extraordinary isolation of spirit which had fallen momentarily upon him. He had told himself it was a dream, a mere fantastic illusion of the brain wrought of the strange atmosphere of the forest; yet, for all that, the memory of the illusion, if such it was, lingered faintly with him, caused him to feel no little relief at the sight of the Castle. Where there is a dwelling, and moreover a lighted dwelling, there are doubtless human beings, and their presence would be of solace to him.

He crossed the grass sward, his feet striking noiselessly on the soft surface. Nearing the windows he looked within. Here he saw a large company seated at a well-furnished board. Glass and silver sparkled on the table. There were decanters full of red wine, dishes piled with fruits, flowers purple, scarlet, and orange. The guests themselves lent brilliance and colour to the scene. Surrounded by a living flower-wreath, so the board appeared; wind-swayed, sun-kissed, as they moved in talk and laughter, jewels on head, neck, and arm glittering in the light.

At the head of the board sat a woman in a robe of orange silk. Her hair, a tawny gold, bound with a fillet of flaming stones, shone with its own lustre, rivalled successfully the brilliance of her gown. Her skin, olive hued, glowed with a very subtle warmth. You guessed her body possessed of the fires of the South. Her eyes, a purple-blue, looked at you from beneath dark brows level and very beautifully marked. Her mouth, curved and modelled like a Greek mouth, squared faintly at the corners, showing her luxurious. Her nose, straight and finely chiselled, had delicately arched nostrils. She leaned back in her chair, a great one of carved ivory, and smiled at the faces around her.

One man sprang to his feet, a pretty youth in purple doublet and hose, a big amethyst hanging from a silver chain about his neck.

"To Thaïs!" he cried, raising his glass on high. The light shining through it the wine glowed like a ruby.

The flower-wreath about the table swayed, rose.

"To Thaïs!" came the cry from a score of voices, while ruby-red glasses flashed aloft.

"The glorious Thaïs!" cried one.

"The divine Thaïs!"

"The adorable Thaïs!"

"The incomparable Thaïs!"

"Thaïs the Enchantress!"

"Thaïs our Venus!"

"Thaïs our Aphrodite!"

"Thaïs whom we worship!"

So the litany went around the board. And Peregrine without mocked in his heart, deeming them fools, yet in a manner envying them their folly.

The cry died away. Again the guests were seated at the table. Peregrine drew his tabor from beneath his cloak, a long sombre garment, given him by an old woman on the third day of his journeying.

"'Tis not well to blazon yourself Jester," she had said sagely. "An' men have the sense to see you so beneath the cloak 'tis other matter. A true Jester will hide his motley. 'Tis your false fool shows his garb to all comers. You, I think, are true Jester." Whereupon she had chuckled very cunningly.

So Peregrine wore the cloak she had given him, finding wisdom in her words. Now from beneath it he pulled forth his tabor, stepped into the shadow of the Castle, touched the strings lightly and set himself to sing.

Listen all who fain would know
How a rose began to grow,
Of its blooming I will show,
None can so well as I.

Planted by a tender smile,
Watered with fair words the while,
Who could guess they were but guile?
None truly less than I.

Soft it opened in the sun;

Never such a perfect one
Bloomed, I wot, since time begun.
None held so true as I.

Red the rose and passing sweet,
For a lady's bosom meet,
There he laid it at her feet.
None saw so well as I.

But she crushed it 'neath her tread,
Bruised and broke it till it bled;
In the mire it lay, dead, dead.
None laughed as soft as I.

Roses red and roses white,
Fragrant, full of sweet delight,
One day's bloom, then falls the night.
None see it dark as I.

Pluck the roses for your own;
Never to another shown
Crush them soon as fully blown.
None warn you well as I.

The song died away. A figure moved to the window. Backed by brilliant light it made a dark patch in the square opening.

"Who sings warningly of love?" demanded a voice.

"I do," said Peregrine through the darkness.

"And who are you, if one may be allowed the question?"

"A wanderer."

"Truly one who has wandered to good purpose since he finds himself at so fair a goal. Wilt show yourself, Sir Wanderer?"

Peregrine stepped into the square of light cast upon the grass from the window. He saw looking out at him a big man clad in scarlet, somewhat full-bodied. His face, as well as Peregrine could see it against the light, was sufficiently humorous, with small twinkling eyes deep-set.

"What brought you hither?"

"Fate an' it please you," returned Peregrine. "Folly an' it like you better."

"Folly leads not on so good a path. We will call it Fate."

"At your will."

"Or perchance it were better to term it good sense."

"Good sense," said Peregrine, "having forethought in plenty gives the surplus of her wares to those she takes in hand. By which token I doubt me 'twas hers led me hither."

The big man laughed. "We'll quarrel not as to the guide. 'Tis good enough that you are here."

"Humph!" said Peregrine, "maybe. But now that I am here what comes next in order?"

"That you enter the Castle."

"A very friendly suggestion," quoth Peregrine. "I would however point out that I bring no letter of credentials."

The big man laughed again, this time rather queerly. "For that matter the fact that you have found your way hither is in itself full enough credential. We are not inhospitable. Also I might suggest that you have no credential from us."

Peregrine shrugged his shoulders. "'Twere a pretty thing if a beggar should demand credentials from the man who gave him alms, or the wanderer from the man who offered him a shelter. An' he did so he were a fool might well go drown in his own folly."

"And you would swim in your own wisdom, so your words and song would show."

"If you judge by words you judge ill," said Peregrine dryly, "since no man will own his words folly. It needs your wise man to own himself a fool, and thereby show his greater wisdom, since he but owns to the heritage of his birth. And the man who denies himself possessed of parents is a very patent fool. But to cease quibbling and come to fact. You see before you a hungry man, a tired man, a foot-sore man. An' your hospitality be of deed rather than word I prithee let me experience it on the instant."

"With all the will in the world," said the big man, and he turned from the window.

The next instant the Castle door was flung wide open. Light streamed blazing forth. Peregrine stumbled towards it. Blinking he found himself atop the steps, dazzled by the greater brilliance.

The man in scarlet caught him by the arm.

"You are spent," he said kindly.

"It would seem so," said Peregrine, laughing ruefully.

"Drink this." A glass of wine was held to his lips.

Peregrine pushed it aside. "An' I drink wine on an empty stomach you will see a very drunken man."

"Bah! 'tis not so potent." Then as Peregrine still pushed the glass aside, "'Tis our custom, man. All who enter here drink a toast to the Lady Thaïs on the doorstep, swear her fealty in drinking."

"You told me not of stipulations," muttered Peregrine very weary.

"'Tis but an ancient custom, man. There's no ill in the glass. Drink it, and cry to Thaïs. 'Twill put new strength into you."

Thus urged Peregrine took the glass. "To Thaïs!" he said, and sipped the wine. Very sweet to the palate it ran warm down his throat. "The divine Thaïs!" he cried laughing, remembering the toast he had heard. He drank the remainder at a draught, flung the glass to the floor. "Ah!" he said. "It puts new life in a man. Your name?" he asked on a sudden of the other.

"They call me Phrixus," came the answer, "since as a child I escaped from my stepmother, a very sharp-tongued woman. Truly 'twas by the skin of my teeth I did so, and on no golden-fleeced ram neither. Phrixus I have been since, and still am. May I ask a name for a name?"

"Peregrine, at your service. A fool as I dare swear myself. A wanderer as you have perceived."

"A lucky wanderer," quoth the other, and took him by the arm. Very gently he propelled him towards the great hall.

Pausing a moment on the threshhold Peregrine looked around. The hall was a riot of colour, a very feast for the sight. A huge place it was; the centre a great domed arch, golden and set on four columns of black marble. The walls were hung with tapestries orange and yellow, bordered with blue and purple most deftly intermingled. So remote were the tapestries that the figures at the table appeared backgrounded against sunlight above deep waters. Around were marble statues, works of the world in the morning of time. Here was Hebe young and slender; Mercury wing-footed; Atalanta poised swift to run; Faunus half man half goat; Bacchus vine-wreathed;

Apollo, Athene, Venus,—all were there wrought of voluptuous fancy. Here and there gleamed silver nymphs and dryads, flashing to seeming life in the red light of the fire which blazed at the further end of the great hall. Green marble made the floor, spread with rugs an harmonious blend of colour. Beneath the golden dome was set the board, and here was movement, life, and laughter.

As Peregrine stood in the doorway with Phrixus beside him, those opposite it looked up and saw him, the others turned.

"Welcome the new-comer!" The cry rang through the hall, losing itself in echoes in the golden dome. None could mistake the genuine ring of it. Peregrine was led forward; kneeling he kissed the hand Thaïs gave him.

"We bid you welcome, Sir," she said very graciously. And she gave him a place on her right.

"Will you not lay aside your cloak?" The request very delicately toned yet held a faint air of command. Willy-nilly Peregrine slipped it from his shoulders.

"Ha!" laughed Phrixus, "you are Jester. So I might have guessed. Truly being so you are doubly welcome. Is it not so, friends?"

Again a cry rang loud. "Welcome the Jester!"

"An' I were not very sure I were waking I should hold myself dreaming," mused Peregrine inwardly. Fate to his mind played pretty pranks with a man's life, tossed it shuttlecock-like from depths to heights, threw it from fair earth to stony ground, and then again to very flowery beds. Here at least was one sufficiently pleasing for the moment. Truly he would take no thought for the morrow, but enjoy the hour to its full. An honoured guest he sat there, satisfying his appetite very fully from silver dishes served to him by pages in white and gold.

The meal ended the board was cleared. It and the trestles on which it lay were carried away by serving men, rugs rolled aside. At the end of the hall, somewhat near the great fireplace, was a raised dais. Here the ivory chair was placed. Thaïs seated in it the company disposed themselves around her according to will. Peregrine lay at her feet on sapphire blue cushions soft as eiderdown. Very content with the present he waited for the next move.

It came. The lights in the hall were extinguished. The moonlight, falling through the windows, lay along the floor in a silver pathway. The tapestries at the further end of the hall swung apart. From between them, down the moonlight path, ran bare-footed girls silken-robed, veiled, four phalanxes of colour, pale heliotrope shading to deepest purple; red to fullest crimson; the green of young beech leaves to the black green of pine trees; maize-colour toning through orange to tawny brown. A moment they swayed bowing before the dais, then set themselves to dance, accompanied by music from hidden musicians. Their feet upon the green marble of the floor were like little white flowers dancing in breeze-swept meadows. Here was very intoxication of movement, rhythm perfect in harmony. As they danced they raised their veils. Peregrine looked on their faces oval, bright-eyed, scarlet-lipped; small heads set on slim young throats. The very incarnation of youth and joy was personified in the dance before him. The fleetness of it, the dainty fragility, brought with it a sense of evanescence. The thought struck suddenly cold to his heart.

Thaïs bent from her chair towards him.

"How does it please you?" she asked, her breath soft upon his cheek, her voice like the tone of a muffled silver bell.

"Madam, it pleases me exceeding well," said Peregrine. Meeting her eyes he smiled.

CHAPTER XIV

THE QUEST

FOR the space of twelve months Peregrine abode at the Castle Syrtes. During the first six the life within it pleased him exceeding well. There was no lack of hospitality; his presence was very assuredly desired. On all sides he found himself a favourite, from the least of the guests to the divine Thaïs herself. This was enough to please a man who had found himself hitherto, save for a few weeks of delusion, of very small importance.

He became Head of the Council of Arts as they termed it, wherein his opinion was most widely deferred to. The Cult of the Jester was on all tongues. What precisely this Cult was I know not, save that it had for its motto *Dum vivimus, vivamus*; and that said it is perchance unnecessary to seek further light on the matter. I know they talked very blandly of Sorrow as the highest exponent of Art, whereas no one of them had ever glimpsed even the fringe of her garment, though Peregrine assuredly believed he had. Joy, they contended, followed close in her path. They spoke intimately of both. But it is very certain that none who have not met Sorrow face to face can hope to meet Joy. Of them all Peregrine was the only one whom we may believe laughed now and again at himself. A very small grace truly, but we may trust a saving one.

For six months, then, he enjoyed himself mightily, held his Council of Arts wherein his speeches were most largely adorned with flowery rhetoric; sang to the ladies in the garden, and heard their praises of his songs very complacently; ate delicate food; drank rare wines; watched dances wherein harmony, rhythm, and colour lent every lure to please the senses. At the end of six months he began to weary, and for the succeeding three stifled mental yawns to the best of his ability. Now and again pleasure would rekindle only to die away to dull ashes. For the last three of the twelve months he was heartily sick of his life as it was, but custom by now having wedded him to the Castle he was somewhat loth to leave. Also, having in mind the memory of his travels before he reached the Castle, he saw not to what end he should depart. Therefore he dallied. He disguised his weariness and dislike of the over-soft life well. None suspected what he thought. It was at this time he had a dream, which brought his dilatory spirit to action.

One noontide, lying in the garden with the autumn sun striking full upon him, he drowsed to slumber. At first, through the slumber, he was conscious of where he lay, felt the warmth of the sun upon his cheek; was aware, though with closed eyes, of the forest which hemmed in the Castle on all sides. Gradually consciousness lost its hold upon him, he slid into a deep silence whence all externals left him. Then it was that the dream came to him. With no beginning he found himself in the midst of it. This is what he dreamed.

He dreamed that he was walking on the far white road climbing the hillside, the same that he had seen a year agone. The sun beat hotly upon it, burning his face, causing the blood in his temples to drum madly. In front of him he saw a figure, a cloaked woman moving swiftly over the road before him. He strained every nerve in pursuit of her, but for all his straining she kept ever ahead. The road became steeper, the sun beat more fiercely upon him. Yet his desire to reach the figure before him was so intense that he would not have halted if he could. But he could not. He knew that till he reached her he must keep ever onward. Then beyond her he saw the tree, its withered branches flung cross-like from the dead trunk. And on a sudden he knew that unless he gained her before she had passed it by he would never reach her. He tried to run and could not, his feet were leaden. He could only keep on at the same dull pace. He saw her now within a yard of the tree. She had gained it. Some cry burst from his throat, half prayer, wholly imploring. At the very foot of the tree she stopped and turned. With laboured steps he came abreast her. He saw her face....

He woke trembling. The dream had been very vivid. Yet more vivid than heat or fatigue was the face of the woman he had seen. Of one thing he was very certain. It was no dream face only. Somewhere the woman was in existence, and from that moment till life should be ended for him he must seek her. If in sleep the desire to reach her had been intense, the desire in waking was threefold. Here one might say was madness and illusion. Maybe. Nevertheless it stung him quick to action.

He got to his feet, picking up his cloak from the ground where it had lain beside him. He looked around. There was no man in sight. So much the better, since he was in no mood either for argument or farewell.

Leaving the smooth green of the grass sward he plunged straight into the forest. Here he was to experience some of that so-called evil magic which brought the forest its ill name. Verily an' he were so minded he might have believed the trees and shrubs possessed of demons so venomously did they seek to bar his passage among them. Knowing, however, the thought sheer foolishness he but mocked at it, and put it from him. The path by which he had made his way to the Castle had become overgrown during his twelve months' sojourn there. The difficulty of his return route fretted him while it roused him to do combat with it. Now and again he paused to break off some branch tough as leather, requiring the full strength of both his hands to twist. He became hot and weary, and very assuredly angry with the difficulties that beset him. A dogged obstinacy took hold on him. For the moment he lost sight of the memory of his dream and the quest on which it had brought him. Sheer determination to win through the forest at any hazard sent him struggling onward. An' he had to break his way piecemeal through the forest he would win his way out. You see him now a very stubborn man, one not to be kept prisoner against his own will and pleasure.

Yard by yard he made his way forward. His hands began to drop blood, his clothes were sadly torn. Two thirds of the forest lay behind him. An' he could hold out for the remainder all were well. He shook the blood from his fingers which smarted very painfully, cried courage to his heart, and beat onward. Here it was that the memory of his dream returned to him, and further, here was the pity of it, returned merely as dream. That was discouraging. It made him appear a fool for his pains, his trouble to no purpose. For a moment his heart cried to him to give up the remainder of his journey, to return on his path.

"Nay," he said, very dogged, "'tis a low suggestion to make a man. An' I return 'tis like as not the reality of the dream returns also. The journey thus far will have been for naught, and it will be but to make again. I cry onward." Which methinks sound reasoning.

Stumbling, bruised, and bleeding he made the last bit of the forest; saw at length the sky between the trees. Worn out he dropped on their margin, halting for a moment's breathing space. While he lay breathless and panting the face of his vision returned to him clear and vivid. Again he knew it for no dream. This much at least he had as reward for his labours. He got to his feet on the instant. The land around him lay in sunshine. Now he saw what had escaped him formerly in the dusk, a path through the bog around the forest. He took it gladly and came out upon the plain. Here in the sunlight he saw the great boulders, less ominous now than in the gathering storm; and far off he saw the white road climbing the hillside. He knew it for his goal without doubt, and set off thither.

An hour or so brought him to it, and he began to ascend. He felt the heat of the sun upon him, bringing his dream clear to mind. Each moment he thought to see the figure on the road before him, but it stretched onward empty up the hill.

He climbed steadily; anon saw the tree dark against the blue of the sky. He pressed forward towards it. So sure had he been at the beginning of the climb of finding what he sought that disappointment fell very hard upon him when he saw no figure standing beneath it. Sick at heart he came up to it, looked around. On every side stretched dusty grass, sun-baked and dry; and on ahead, between the stretches of it, passed the white road. The futility of his quest struck upon him. He felt himself a deluded man.

About to turn bitterly away his eye was caught by an impress in the dusty ground below the tree. Bending closer he saw foot-marks, clear and unblurred, deeply imprinted. Someone had stood there not long since. Slight hope to go on, seeing it might have been a mere wayfarer such as he himself. Yet even as a drowning man grips hold on a straw so Peregrine gripped on the faint hope the impress brought him. He saw now that the marks passed on along the road. With hope renewed he followed in their track.

CHAPTER XV

SIMON OF THE BEES

IN a valley, hill-surrounded on all sides, with but a narrow passage between them to the north and to the south, stood on a time a hamlet. It clustered for the most part round the parish church, a small building, with a square low tower at one end. For all I know it stands there to this day, though most assuredly the houses then around it are done away with. This fact, an' I were so minded, might lead me to inscribe sage reflections on the decay of life, and the passing of time. But I am by no means disposed so to weary you, for which mercy you will doubtless cry *Deo gratias*, or some such pious thanks. My business is merely to chronicle Peregrine's wanderings on his quest, and to leave sage reflections to those more apt to deal with them.

Winter lay over the valley at this time. Snow massed upon the roads making them well-nigh impassable. Wise folk ventured not far afield, but, returning from enforced expeditions with speed, made themselves snug between four walls. Round the same walls the wind blew shrilly.

Within one of the cottages an old man sat crouched over a turf fire. A wizened old thing he was, his face crossed and recrossed with wrinkles, till it was like a withered brown apple. He stretched gnarled old hands to the blaze, hands hardened with many years of holding a spade. Folk said his heart was as hard as his hands. It may be they spoke truth. It is certain that if he had a heart, hard or soft, he kept it very well hidden. None speaking a good word of him, he spoke a good word of none. Give and it shall be given you, was his motto; which being interpreted meant, An' you give to me, I will e'en give to you, an interpretation other than is usual to it. The motto was not likely to bring him any vast satisfaction, though doubtless he cheated himself into imagining that it did. At all events it was the one he had chosen, and that to his mind stood for something. You will perceive, too, that through it he saw himself against mankind, not mankind against him; that also stood for something. In his way he was a bit of a thinker. None knew this for certain, as he kept his thoughts, if he had any, to himself; but he was suspected of them. This was not in his favour. Thinking is for your student, your philosopher, your priest, possibly for your lord of the manor. It comes not into the life of a villain. Work, food, and sleep; sleep, food, and work are in the natural order of things; mayhap a prayer or two to Our Lady and the saints, and at the last, death, which, being more pitiful than life, is not ill welcome.

He had no kith nor kin; no one and nothing for which he cared, save his bees. Of these he had a goodly store, ten hives set in the garden behind his hovel,—it was little else. In the summer they made music around him while he tilled the soil. He found their droning very pleasant to his ears. By virtue of this goodly possession he was called Simon of the Bees. The title was dear to him, though no man dreamed it. Here was the sole thing mankind had ever bestowed on him which afforded him pleasure; yet, since the bestowal was of careless custom rather than of charity aforethought, it was deserving of no reward. Such was his reasoning. It was a matter of occasional speculation in the village as to whom Simon would will his bees on his death, having no kin. It remained, however, speculation; and was like to do so.

On this winter night Simon, warming his hands over the fire, and muttering now and again to himself, was roused from his muttering by a blow on the door. He got slowly to his feet, grumbling the while, and drew back the wooden bolt which made it fast. Without, in the darkness, he saw a cloaked figure standing in the wind-driven snow.

"Shelter, for the love of heaven," said a man's voice.

"I am none so sure of the love," responded Simon, and made to shut the door. In this he was frustrated by the sudden swaying of the figure, which fell very prone across his threshhold, feet and legs without, head and shoulders on the mud floor of the hovel.

"A very unceremonious entry," grumbled Simon. And he stood for a moment irresolute. The man could not lie where he was, since his bulk upon the step made it impossible to close the door. The wind blew the smoke in eddying waves about the room. In a moment you could scarce see a hand's breadth before your face. To push him without meant his death on a very certainty. Directly or indirectly Simon had never yet had the murder of a man on his soul, whatever sins else burdened it. Grumbling more heartily he got his hands under the man's arms, and tugged him forward into the room. Then he made the door fast again.

The smoke now making its way through the hole in the roof, the air cleared somewhat. Simon looked down upon the prostrate figure.

"An' he dies within 'twere e'en less pleasant than he died without," he muttered. He got water in a horn cup, and held it to the man's lips, forcing it between them. In a moment or so the man opened his eyes, lifted himself feebly on his elbow, and looked around.

"Where am I?" he asked.

"No more original than the rest of men," muttered Simon. "There never yet was swooning man but asked his whereabouts on coming to himself. Doubtless fearing to find himself in a less pleasant place than he is accustomed to. An' you would know, you are in the shelter you demanded."

"I thank you."

Simon shrugged his shoulders. "No thanks are due. You forced an entry."

"You might have pushed me without."

"And have had your death on my soul. 'Twould be a heavier burden than I've a mind for." He seated himself again by the fire. The man watched him from the floor.

"Who you are I know not," said Simon, "where you come from I care less, but that you must bide here the night is obvious."

"I am rejoiced you see it so," was the reply. "My name is Peregrine, a Jester, at your service. Since I bide here the night 'twere well we were acquainted, in spite of your little caring."

Simon grunted. "A Jester! A pretty jest it would have been for me an' you had died on my threshhold. What caused you swoon?"

"Hunger," said Peregrine very simply.

Simon looked at him from beneath shaggy eyebrows. Then he got slowly to his feet. From a shelf he fetched a plate of dark bread.

"Eat," he said briefly, holding it towards him.

Peregrine fell ravenously upon the coarse food. A moment Simon watched him, then turned again to the shelf. From it he took a piece of honeycomb.

"Here," he said gruffly, "'tis toothsome stuff."

Peregrine took it from him. "I thank you heartily," he made reply. Simon grunted, and went back to his seat. From it he watched Peregrine devour the bread and honeycomb, lick his fingers of the sticky sweetness. The simple meal finished, Peregrine looked across at his host.

"Will you give me your name?" asked Peregrine.

"Simon of the Bees, men call me," was the reply given with a regal carelessness. Neither the regality, nor the would-be carelessness of the answer escaped Peregrine.

"A goodly title," he responded, "to which I am doubtless indebted for a sweet meal."

Simon grunted.

"I like bees," said Peregrine.

Simon grunted again. It was his nearest approach to conversation. Peregrine took it as such.

"Diligent little atoms," pursued Peregrine, "busy on their own pursuits. Faithful too; each choosing its own kind of flower it sticks to it like a true man to his love. Fearing no one, they dislike those that fear them, and show their dislike accordingly."

Simon grunted a third time, but approvingly. He found in Peregrine an observer of his favourites. A silence endured a little space; then Simon put a question showing interest in his guest. This was marvel, had Peregrine but known.

"What brought you hither?"

"Humph!" said Peregrine. "That is none too easy a question to answer. Maybe a dream, maybe a reality. At times I have thought that which brought me on my wanderings but the airy nothingness of which dreams are fashioned; at times I have known it for more, seen in my pursuit the one solid and sane action of my life."

Simon gave vent to his usual grunt. "You tell me little. What is it you pursue?"

"A woman."

"I might have known it." Simon laughed mockingly.

"She is not as other women," said Peregrine musing. "She has quiet eyes."

"Truly!" said Simon.

"I saw her in a dream," went on Peregrine. "Now I seek her."

Again Simon laughed. "On your own showing the quest savours of madness. A woman with quiet eyes, forsooth, once seen in a young man's dream! An' that is all you have to go on, how think you to find her?"

"I know not," said Peregrine very quiet.

"Madness," said Simon crossly.

"Mayhap," smiled Peregrine.

"Sheer madness," said Simon.

"Quite possible."

"Huh!" grunted Simon, and relapsed into silence. Now and again he looked at Peregrine sitting on the mud floor in the dim firelight, his hands clasped round his knees. From him he looked at the fire, then back again at the man. Memory, long sleeping, was struggling to birth in his soul. The lines on his face quivered now and again in its travail. On a sudden he spoke.

"I was once young."

"So are all men once," said Peregrine very softly.

"I too had my dreams," said Simon gruffly.

"They aid a man," said Peregrine.

"Maybe, and maybe not. 'Twill aid a man, mayhap, to have a son and see him grow to manhood. Of what aid is his birth an' he wither of some hidden disease in childhood, suffer and die with none but you to sorrow? To my thinking no hope at all were better than hope unfulfilled."

Peregrine mused, his eyes on the glowing turf. "Methinks I find your simile not over apt. An' a child of our flesh die, we may see God's Hand in the death. An' a hope of our heart die, mayhap we are the murderers."

Simon turned on him half savagely. "Is a mother a murderer that her babe dies in her arms for lack of the milk in her breasts, an' she'd give her life's blood for it would it avail? Methinks you must look somewhat further."

Peregrine was silent. Here he found no answer to give.

"Sixty year and more I've lived here in this hovel," went on Simon, "and never a kindly word spoken to me. I might be the plague itself for the way men eye me. From boyhood 'twas the same. Mayhap 'tis something bred in me they shun. Yet, for all that, I nurtured hope for twenty year; dreamed, as you dream now. At last I had naught left on which to nourish it. It shrivelled and died. I saw it twist in agony, for 'twas no easy death. When it was dead I laughed that it had ever lived. Hope, I tell you, dying in a man's soul rots there, turns his soul foul. Better strangle it before it comes to birth. Then you can rid yourself of it. Later you cannot; and dying it lies there to canker and decay." He stopped, and again Peregrine could find no answer. The wind sighed through the trees without; all else was silence.

"Did you speak?" asked Simon suddenly.

"No," said Peregrine startled, "yet methought———"

"Fancy," said Simon shortly.

"Nay," said Peregrine listening. "It was as a voice from far off places. *Ego sum resurrectio et vita*, it said."

"The wind sighing in the trees brings voices to a man's fancy," returned Simon crossly.

"And yet—" said Peregrine wondering.

"I too have dreamed," retorted Simon. "Hope, I tell you, is dead within my soul. Yet—yet one fancy remains. An' it be not wholly foul, an' there be one spot of sweetness left within it e'er I die, perchance 'twill be carried hence by my singing bees. A mad fancy, and I am e'en mad to dream it. 'Tis cankered through and through. We have had enough of jargon for the time. An' you would sleep, there's your couch." He pointed to a heap of dried bracken in a corner of the room.

Peregrine rose from the floor, crossed to the bracken, and lay down. Simon sat motionless by the fire. Without, the wind sighed among the trees in the valley.

A sound in the room roused Peregrine the next morning. He looked up to see Simon standing by the open doorway. Without, the dim world was carpetted in snow.

"You made good slumber," said Simon turning and seeing him awake.

"Exceeding good," responded Peregrine refreshed and cheerful. "And how fared you?"

"As needful," grunted Simon.

"I must onward," said Peregrine.

"Still mad," grumbled Simon. "You must eat first."

He produced more bread and honeycomb. They mealed in silence. The meal ended, Peregrine got to his feet.

"An' gratitude were substantial reward," he said, "you were very substantially rewarded. 'Tis all I have to offer."

"'Tis rare enough to be appreciated," said Simon very grim.

Peregrine laughed. "I bid you adieu," he said. He had got to the door when Simon came beside him.

"An' you would find her you seek," he said, "seek her in death's chamber. She closes the eyes of the dead."

"What mean you?" asked Peregrine. "You speak in parable."

"No parable; in very truth. She has passed through this village more than once."

"You have seen her, and yet you term me mad," cried Peregrine.

Simon laughed. "I have spoken," he said, and turned within the hovel.

CHAPTER XVI

ILLUSION

THE sun was not yet risen when Peregrine left the cottage. To the west, behind the hills, the sky glowed faintly luminous. Around him the valley lay yet in dusk, through which the trees and bushes reared ghostly arms, white-shrouded, very spectre-like. The air was alive with an intense purity, exceeding still, yet vital.

Away to the right, beyond the church, he saw a square building. A cross crowning it at one end, he judged it the retreat of holy men or women,— monks or nuns. Through the narrow slits of windows came the gleam of pale candlelight, showing the occupants of the building already astir, busy with *Ave* or *Paternoster*, possibly kneeling devout at Mass. Even as he looked a bell rang out, its clear tone piercing the silence. Habit caused him to bow his head. The action was involuntary; he had done with such matters long since, or fancied to have done with them. In either case it comes to the same for the time being. We need not be nice as to the interpolation of a word.

Turning to the south he took the road towards the opening between the hills. It lay, very smoothly white, between a snow-shrouded wall on the one side, and a fence on the other. Now he noticed a single line of footprints in the snow, small and clear, passing on before him. His imagination fired on the instant, he followed in their wake. They led him clean through the village to a pine wood on its outskirts, beyond which lay the route between the hills.

The sun was up by the time he reached its edge, gilding the western sky, flooding the earth with its beams. Following the footsteps he entered the wood, found himself caught in its mystic silence. Here was the brooding stillness, the peace of some vast cathedral. Between the aisles of the pine trees the chequered light straggled but a little way. This emphasized the solitude. The soul of the place seemed withdrawn from sensible light and warmth into a great silence.

Less conscious of the atmosphere around him than of the footsteps he was following, Peregrine pursued his way. A very certain hope beat in his heart. It was perchance less hope than certainty. As he walked he looked not at the trees around him, but at the footprints on the ground. The snow had fallen sparsely between the pines, covering the path but thinly. In the footmarks he could see the brown of the pine needles, and here and there a glint of green moss. For the space of some half hour he walked; the wood extended further than he had believed on entering it. On either hand he saw the tracks of tiny feet, of birds, of mice, of rabbits. Down a glen gleamed the berries of a rowan tree, scarlet against the darkness of the pines. A few fallen berries below it shone blood-red on the snow.

At length he gained the further outskirts of the wood, came into full sunshine. Here was moorland stretching upward right and left to the hills; before him it narrowed to the pass between them. Some hundred yards or so ahead of him he saw a rude cottage, mud-walled, thatched with rushes and bracken. It stood solitary in the expanse of snow. The footprints led towards it. You may be very sure that Peregrine followed the footprints.

Coming up to the cottage he peered through the small square opening that served for window. Now verily his heart beat to suffocation. This is what he saw.

The middle of the floor held a rough bier; a coarse linen sheet was drawn over that which lay upon it. Two candles stood at the head, their flame pale and insignificant in the sunshine which fell through the window. He did not mark a woman sleeping at the far end of the room, lying, most evidently exhausted, on a heap of moss and skins. His eyes were all for a veiled figure kneeling by the bier. Flashing through his mind came Simon's words.

"Seek her in death's chamber. She closes the eyes of the dead."

You may well believe his heart cried, "At last!" The weary months of his quest sank from him. He had found her. Past difficulties had vanished; past fatigue was forgotten in present rest; past heart-burning in present happiness. He dared not yet make his presence known. It was enough that there she knelt, her head bowed towards the bier. You see him humbled. He had doubted his dream at times. It was now embodied before him. Here was enough to bow a man to the earth, to abase his soul, the while joy raised it high. So for a little space he stood entranced. Going at last to the door, he put his hand upon the latch.

The sound of its raising roused the kneeling woman. She got to her feet. A gentle-faced nun she stood there, looking at the man in the doorway.

"Sir?" she said questioningly, her voice very low.

Peregrine was as one turned to stone. His heart was sick within him.

"Sir," she said again very gently, "what seek you? Here is death present."

Peregrine looked at her. A mad desire to laugh assailed him. Yet courtesy was ever strong upon him.

"Madam, I crave your pardon," he said hoarsely. "I—I have made a mistake." Blindly he turned from the door, stumbled out into the snow.

CHAPTER XVII

APHORISMS

FOR a time Peregrine was as one distraught. It may not be far beside the mark to term him mad. He saw himself in the past mocked by a woman; he saw himself now mocked by a man. In both he saw vaguely the shadow of mockery by a Higher Power. Truly a hard state. Yet strangely, for all that, he lost not hold on his quest. Where heart's desire had urged him in the past, fierce obstinacy now spurred him forward. The face of the woman he sought was ever before his mind. He believed her withheld and hidden from him by conspiring Fate. This roused him to battle. He would move Earth and Heaven and Hell to find her; die, if need be, in the attempt. This you may guess he was very like to do. Already his wanderings had told on him. It was now mid-winter, as we have seen, and that season is not one for e'en the hardiest to be afoot at all times, dependent on chance for shelter.

Of late he had aged considerably. This was not over strange, since age comes not with the mere passing of Time, but with the pressure of his finger in the passing. He had pressed hard on Peregrine. You see him very different from the love-bathed youth, who had sat by the sundial in the flower-scented garden; the joyous youth, who had wandered the fields with Pippo; the wounded youth, who had lain in the wood, his cheek pressed to Mother Earth; the egoist, who had held his Council of Arts in Castle Syrtes; who, dauntless, had fought his way through the forest. He was a man soul-sick, weary, desperate, pursuer of a forlorn hope, so men would term it.

Here it was that a certain duplex side of his character showed itself. One part of his nature would have ranged itself on the side of men, would have stood with them for the madness of his quest, its mere foolishness rather. This part of his nature he strangled very fiercely. Pride had a hand in the strangling. He would make his quest true, prove himself no fool. He saw himself in a sense creator of what he sought. He himself, by virtue of his belief in the woman, would materialize her, if she existed but in realms of fancy. Thus, I say, he would prove himself no fool. This was veritable madness. Yet I have told you Peregrine was for the moment not fully sane.

Leaving the cottage of illusion,—this is what he termed it to himself, and very bitterly,—he had made for the south, to the pass between the hills. Descending for a time, the path had at length led upwards between more pine woods, like to that he had lately traversed. Misery and the whiteness of the snow combined to daze him. He walked like a man in a trance. Subconsciously his mind worked, came to the state I have shown you. In this mood he formed certain aphorisms, some possibly already known by him; some new, created from old material.

"*Cogito, ergo sum,*—I think, therefore I exist," being the first of them it led easily to his second.

"Thought is a creative power. Think deeply, and you will create greatly." *Ergo*, by dwelling with every particle of his mind on the thought of the woman he sought, he would create her.

"Hope is a collective force. Terror and doubt disperse what you have thereby acquired." *Ergo*, hope was the thought by which he would collect material for his creation. To allow terror or doubt to work alongside would be to undertake one of the seven labours of Hercules.

"Desire, being also thought and thereby creative, brings its own attainment." *Ergo*, he desired the woman he sought and would attain to her. This was as certain as that a wheat seed can bring forth nought but wheat. It became, to his mind, a law of Nature. You see each of his aphorisms harping to the same end. Doubtless there were plenty more of them. Those I have given you will suffice.

Coming near the summit of the hill he made out a wayside cross, backgrounded by the pines. It stood weather-beaten and solitary. Here and there the stone was hidden by yellow fungus and grey lichen. Below it knelt a figure. For a breathing space Peregrine felt his heart bound. The next instant he had himself and his heart well under control. No second time would he give way to mere fancy. Here he was very wise. Coming further he saw a little peasant girl, ragged and ill clad. At the foot of the cross she had laid a bunch of holly. She turned on his approach, looking at him with wide childish eyes.

"I give you good-day, sir," she said shyly, as he paused a moment.

"Good-day," responded Peregrine, though in no mood to term it truly good.

"I—I have laid the holly there," she said, as seeing him still stop she sought for conversation.

"A pretty thought," said Peregrine indulgently. It was no more in his nature to snub a child than to strike an animal.

"I often bring flowers," pursued the little maid. "First there are daffodils and primroses to bring. They are very fresh and sweet. Later come bluebells and herb Robert. They are not so pleasant-scented. Next come roses and honeysuckle. They are the most fragrant of all. In the autumn there are always leaves, which are as pretty as flowers, when they are red and gold. Now there is holly."

"That is pretty too," said Peregrine.

"Yes," replied the child. "But it is sad. It is very thorny, and the berries are red like blood. When I see it I think of the crown of thorns, and Christ's death."

"A sorrowful fancy," said Peregrine, and somewhat uneasily.

"'Tis not a fancy," averred the child, discriminating nicely. "'Tis a thought. Fancies may not be over good."

"Truly," smiled Peregrine, finding amusement despite himself at the earnest tone of the small discriminator. "What manner of fancies, may I ask?"

Gravely she surveyed him. There was no mockery in his smile. An' there had been she would have held her peace. Instead she cogitated, seeking to make her meaning clear.

"I know," she said wisely after a moment, "that there are evil spirits in the world. They roam abroad, especially in darkness. I used to fancy we were all safer from their power from Christmas till Ascension Day. I fancied Christ truly on the earth during that time. After Ascension Day He seemed further away, and sometimes I was frighted. I told this to Father Bernard. He said that it was merely fancy. He said Our Lord was ever present now upon the earth in the Blessed Sacrament, in greater glory now than when He lived on earth before. I have forgotten what more he said; but I am no longer frighted when Ascension Day is past. You see, what I held before was fancy, and—and—I cannot tell you rightly, but Father Bernard would show you that fancies are not the same as thoughts."

"Humph!" said Peregrine, having no mind to test the perspicacity of Father Bernard or any other priest on the matter. He hitched his cloak closer around him, ready to start again on his way. The movement disclosed his tabor hanging by a frayed ribbon from his neck. The child saw it; curiosity was quick astir.

"What is that?" she demanded, finger pointing.

"My tabor," returned Peregrine.

"Tabor?" she queried. The word as well as the instrument was unknown to her. "What is a tabor?"

"A musical instrument," said Peregrine, smiling at the little ignoramus.

"Music!" Her eyes sparkled, her cheeks glowed. "Ah, play it!" This was on a note of deep entreaty.

Peregrine shrugged his shoulders. Here was an interlude in his former mood of blackness. It was not wholly distasteful. You have seen that he favoured children. He found quaintness in this one.

"What shall I play for you?" he demanded, unslinging the instrument.

"Play while I sing," she said firmly. "That will sound well."

Peregrine chuckled. "Truly that depends on the singing," quoth he. "On, then, with the song."

Birdlike her voice rose in the pure air. Peregrine catching the melody came in with the tabor. Here is what she sang.

Of one that is so fair and bright

Velut maris stella,

Brighter than the day is light,

Parens et puella:

I cry to thee, thou see to me,

Lady, pray thy Son for me,

Tam pia,

That I may come to thee

Maria.

All this world was forlorn

Eva peccatrice,

Till our Lord was here born

De te genetrice.

With *ave* it went away

Darkling night, and comes the day

Salutis;

The well springeth out of thee,

Virtutis.

Lady, flower of each thing,

Rosa sine spina,

Thou bear'st Jesus, Heaven's King,

Gratia divina:

Of all thou bear'st the prize,

Lady, queen of paradise

Electa:

Maid mild, Mother *es*

Effecta.

"There," she cried triumphant, as she ended, most innocently pleased with the performance, "I said it would sound well."

"Liquid silver notes from a throat of gold," said Peregrine, verily astonished. "An' I had not other matters on hand, you and I might well roam the world together, and men would truly hearken to us, or they are greater dullards than even I judge them."

She looked at him with longing eyes. His words held open a vista of bliss before her. But she shook her head sadly.

"It cannot be. I have work to do," she said sorrowful.

"For that matter so indeed have I," quoth Peregrine. "What manner of work is thine?"

"I mind my father's goats," she responded. "What work is yours?"

"I seek some one," said Peregrine grimly.

"Some one you have lost?"

"Some one I have never found," was the answer.

"Oh," responded the child perplexed. Then shyly, "I must be about my work. I thank you, sir. God speed you with your seeking." Waiting for no response she nodded to him, turned off into the pinewood.

Peregrine went slowly on his way.

The interlude had come happily. There is a healthful sanity in a child's company, even if it endure but a brief space. Peregrine felt his mind somewhat cleansed of the murkiness which had enshrouded it. He began to picture the woman he sought as present with him. This eased his mind for a while, even though it tantalized. It lifted him to a more exalted mood. He identified her with the Spirit of Life around him, saw her passing over the snow swift-footed, fancied her coming from among the pines towards him, heard her voice in the light breeze which stirred them. He held her thus in his thought throughout the day. He saw her image in the glowing sunset, fancied the purpling light across the hills the spreading of her veil. So far so good. With the night, fatigue descended on him. There comes a point in this state when fancy cannot readily be embraced, nor even held though formerly present. Reality is required upon which to rest the mind. This Peregrine had not. Fancy slipping from him left him desolate. He was also very hungry. Fate had thrown no dwelling in his path whereat he could beg bread. Therefore he had not broken his fast since early morning. The needs of nature joining with desolation of mind to bear him down, he found himself heavily weighted.

Darkness lay around him. The sky, which at close of sunset had clouded, brought very meagre light to guide him. Only the faint glimmer of the white road before him gave him his route. He stumbled on, sinking at times knee deep in the snow, where it lay drifted beneath the wall.

The wind began to rise, and with it feathery flakes came silent and insidious. They touched his cheek like soft cold kisses. You would never have dreamed danger in their tenderness. They came faster, thicker. The wind swirled them in a dancing maze. A few steps further, and a blizzard was upon him. The wind rushing from the north smote him that he could barely stand. The snow leaped and flashed around him, blinding, suffocating. He staggered on doggedly.

"An' I stop now I never find her." That was his thought, barely articulate even to his own mind.

In his stress forgotten habit came to him. A prayer rose to his lips. He put it swift aside. Long ago he had prayed, believed in prayer, in God, in a woman he had created,—a woman who had prayed. She had mocked at him; cast him from her. Therefore he had put her and her beliefs from him, and with them his own, being like to hers. In this you see sheer stupidity, and rightly. The Creator is not responsible for hypocrisy in His creatures. That is where the Devil comes in with his handling of matters. This Peregrine had not seen formerly, nor was like to do so now, blinded and stupefied as he was by his conflict with the snow.

Putting prayer aside, then, he trusted to his own efforts. It is certain that he lacked not courage of a kind. His arm up shielding his face, he struggled on. His breath came in sobbing gasps. A dark mass looming before him brought him to a halt. From out the mass gleamed a faint light piercing the snow-driven atmosphere. He took a step towards it, and sank in a drift to his thigh. For a moment he struggled, but to sink the deeper. Well-nigh spent, drowsiness was falling on him. It seemed that further effort availed him nought. As well rest now as not; rest and sleep.

In the blinding snow around him he thought he saw a woman standing. She came nearer, bending to him. Now indeed he cried, "At last!" and stretched out his arms. Even as he cried, he saw her eyes. They were avenging, terrible.... The snow was like a white flame round her....

Shuddering with more than cold, he looked full at her. Then unconsciousness fell upon him.

CHAPTER XVIII

THE SAGE

MENIPPUS LACHESIS, sitting in his turret chamber, was poring over a parchment. You may be very sure this was not the name with which his parents had started him in life. It was with one simpler. I have heard it rumoured that once on a time he was known as Thomas Herdman,—a good honest appellation truly. That time, however, was now many years old, and rumour can easily go astray; indeed, rumour wandering from the mark more often than not, there is little credence to be put in that quarter. At all events it is sufficient for our purpose that he was now known as above set forth,—Menippus Lachesis, the Sage, reader of the riddle of the stars, gazer of crystals, philosopher of numbers, and penetrator into the secrets of life. Many men sought his wisdom, and if they left him little the wiser, through the multiplicity of his words or the brevity of his cryptic utterances, either of which was given them according to their needs as figured by Menippus, that doubtless was due to their own lack of receptiveness.

The turret chamber was a circular room hung with twelve blue curtains. To the north the curtains were indigo; they then passed through shades of sapphire to a clear light blue at the south, and back again through sapphire blue to indigo. Here you have shown the darkness of the winter months, lightening through spring to summer, and back again to the darkness of winter. Each curtain was embroidered in gold with its own sign of the Zodiac, from the Ram, through the rest of them to the Fishes.

On the table near him, lying on black velvet the better to avoid reflections, was an egg-shaped crystal. A pretty enough thing it was, with its smooth surface clear and very luminous, true rock crystal, wherein your least initiated may gaze with advantage, so termed. For my part, I will take leave to question the advantage. By the crystal stood a gold vessel, cup-shaped, quaintly wrought with devices, of which the most obvious was the pentagram. It held a purplish liquid of the consistency of ink.

The room had no windows. At all times it was lighted by a small hanging lamp, two gold wings bearing between them a red glass holding oil and a burning wick. For the better lighting of the place when the Sage was at his studies, there were a couple of candles set in bronze candlesticks.

Menippus, reading from the parchment, paused now and again to peer into the gold cup, or look a moment towards the crystal. That some weighty matter was under consideration might be judged by the wrinkling of his brow, and the tapping of his clawlike finger on the table. A tall man, this Menippus, he looked the part himself, or Fate, had given him exceeding well. His hair, white and plentiful, fell straight on either side his face, and to the nape of his neck. His moustache and beard were of glossy silkiness. The latter, pointed, touched the third button of his black gown fashioned not unlike a priest's cassock, the sleeves only being somewhat wider and looser. Round his neck hung a gold chain, and from it a gold device. The centre thereof was a small cross set within a triangle. Without the triangle was a circle, and without the circle a second triangle.

On the forefinger of his right hand he wore a large seal ring, the setting blackened silver, the seal itself very ancient, reddish stone, carved with devices as follows: Man in his potential divinity (I give the reading Menippus would have given you) before the Fire Altar, backed by the Pillar of Truth, and looking towards the Trinity (Pagan), Man, Woman, and Child: these three surmounted by the Supreme,—a Woman crowned with the Sun; behind her, the Cornucopia, before her, the Caduceus; behind the Pillar of Truth, the Crescent Moon, horns pointing upwards; above it, a seven-pointed star. About his head he wore a thin gold fillet, in the centre was placed a Rising Sun. To those versed in such matters the sun, the ring, and the symbol at his breast showed him as belonging to the Ancient Order of Lux. An exceeding ancient Order this, Egyptian, and dating from far beyond the time of Solomon.

Where and how Menippus received his initiation into this Order was a mystery, but that his initiation was more than the mere wearing of the symbols of the Order, he proved in vastly more ways than one. The few who came to his tower to leave it with greater knowledge than was contained in multiplicity of words and brief cryptic utterances, left it with sealed lips, but with hearts wherein awe and dread were strangely intermingled. Such power as Menippus showed them was unquestionably power, but whence it came was another matter.

A high-nosed, thin-lipped man he was, his face yellow like the parchments he studied. His eyes, black as sloes, and very piercing, were set beneath shaggy eyebrows. The lids of them folding far back at his will, left them at times staring and unblinking. This gave them an hypnotic power. At other times, when in deep thought, they cut across the pupil of the eye; then you saw the eyes heavy-lidded. This alteration of the eyelids' form was a marked characteristic of his. It set the hearts of curious women—those who sought his wisdom—a-beating; more than once sent them scuttling like frightened hens to the door, and adown the stairs, while Menippus sat chuckling cynically. Weak enough to desire his power to be sought and acknowledged by all men, mere curiosity bored him vastly. You may judge that he was more often bored by his visitors than not. Vanity alone made boredom worth the enduring. It was a strange quality to find in a man of his age and power. Pride and unscrupulousness one might well expect; but here was a strain of weakness running through his strength, one which had endured from his earliest years. It is perchance needless to say that but for it he would have been greater than he was, and he was no small man intellectually no more than physically. This same vanity had led him into works no man dare even name with impunity.

Turning now from the parchment before him, he fetched a deep sigh, let his gaze rest ardently on the crystal. Now you see the heavy lids cutting the pupils in a straight line. An' you had seen more, had seen with those same heavy-lidded black eyes, you would have seen the crystal cloud to milkiness, first a mere drop in its clearness, spreading gradually across the whole. The cloudiness gave way to light, sudden and brilliant, at first many-hued as a rainbow, then turning to a clear whiteness. Across the whiteness rode a ship full-sailed. Here was the definite signal of on-coming vision. Next, and you must take the vision with what credence you may, he saw a man struggling through a snowstorm, blinded, dazed. He watched more closely. Could you have read his mind, you would have known the sight not unexpected. It held the interpretation to certain cryptic utterances in the parchment spread before him. I do not pretend to understand how these things may be; I but give you as plainly as I am able all that chanced on that night of snow and storm, and that which followed after. With the powers that leagued together in the handling of the matter I desire no dealing. An' the whole happening had not close bearing on the history of Peregrine it might well be omitted. Being, however, close bound with him at the moment, and with that which was to befall him later, it is incumbent on me, and I would be a fair chronicler, to set it plainly forth. In the crystal, then, Menippus saw a man struggling through the snow, saw him coming ever nearer, saw him sink at last as we have seen him. At this the vision was obliterated. Returning to concrete surroundings, he saw the crystal lying on the black velvet, catching the glow from the hanging lamp, naught else pictured within it.

Menippus got quickly to his feet, made his way to the door.

"Castrano," he called.

A huge negro came silently from behind a curtain.

"Come on the instant," said Menippus. "I need your aid. A man lies in a snow-drift without."

CHAPTER XIX

THE CHOICE

PEREGRINE, returning to consciousness, and unaware at the first of his surroundings, believed the snow to be an exceeding warm bed. This being so he lay still a while, very grateful for the repose to his aching limbs. Anon he opened his eyes, saw above him a dark arched roof, over which light flickered, saw before him the steady flame of a small lamp. This phenomena struck him as curious to find in a snow-drift, brought him to further investigation. Now he found that he lay not on snow, but on a couch, soft and luxurious, warm covering spread over him. Marvelling greatly he turned his head, found himself in a room, saw the flickering light to come from a wood fire on a great hearth.

By the hearth a man was sitting reading from a large book propped on a stand before him. Behind him was a shelf holding bottles, crucibles, and other glass vessels, some containing dark shapes, exceeding unpleasant to look upon. On three pedestals stood three figures; Clotho, who according to the Ancients spins the Thread of Life; Lachesis, who sees to its guiding, and whom Menippus had taken for his patroness; Atropus, who cuts it when she and her sisters will. Peregrine looked at this last with interest. He fancied she had but lately had her shears in hand for him, frustrated only by her sister, Lachesis. In this thought he possibly shot pretty near the mark.

Then he saw that Menippus had turned towards him, was surveying him gravely, the while one skinny finger kept the place in his book.

"So you have come to yourself," said Menippus.

"I have evidently you to thank as my rescuer," said Peregrine struggling to his elbow.

"Lie still," said Menippus briefly. "It is sometimes doubtful whether thanks are due in such a matter. On this occasion, however, believing that you owe them, I accept them from you. It were well that you rested for a time. I would, however, converse with you. What brought you hither?"

"Foolishness," said Peregrine very dryly.

"There I take leave to differ from you," remarked Menippus. "Curiosity or wisdom might have led you an' you had come of set purpose. Believing neither to have had a hand in the matter, I see rather the guidance of my patroness Lachesis." Turning he bowed towards one of the three figures.

"Truly," smiled Peregrine ruefully, "her sister had her shears ready to the thread."

"Ha! you recognize them. That is well. Yet, despite the guidance of Lachesis, I can fancy you imagined some guidance of your own?"

"Rather the guidance of a myth I pursued to my own undoing," said Peregrine.

"There again I must make correction," remarked Menippus very suavely. "Whatever myth you pursued, you pursued it to your advantage, since it led you hither."

"Have it your own way," laughed Peregrine, "I am too weary to do combat with you."

Menippus took his finger out of the book and leaned back in his chair. He looked gravely at Peregrine. There was a note in the laughter which showed less respect than he considered his due. Briefly, his vanity, a tender commodity, was pricked.

"Putting for the nonce," he said, "laughter aside, I would have you speak more plainly. Show me shortly the myth you pursued."

Here was a slight air of command, which for a moment stung the Jester. The next, humour prevailed. He saw matter for amusement in the evident seriousness of the other. It was plain that he took himself by no means lightly.

"Well," quoth Peregrine, "since you desire brevity in the account you shall have it. I had a dream, a vision, call it what you will."

"What manner of vision?" demanded Menippus.

"The vision of a woman," replied Peregrine. "Though it was but in vision I saw her, I believed her to exist in reality, hence I set out to find her. I have pursued her for over a year. Plainly, I know not truly whether she exists or no. At times I have been certain of her reality; at times the certainty has fallen from me. A moment or so agone it had left me. Now, in speaking of her again, I am very sure she lives. There is the matter in a nutshell. 'Tis a tantalizing enough quest for a man, and maybe I am a fool to pursue it. At times I see the folly very plainly, at times I see in it naught but the clearest sanity."

Menippus drew down his eyelids. His finger-tips together he spoke smoothly.

"Presuming the quest sane, presuming it fulfilled, what think you to gain when you have found her?"

"That," said Peregrine quietly, "will lie between her and me." The Sage's tone had struck strangely on his heart. It brought with it at once hope and danger. Here it is none too easy to make my meaning clear. It was as though, on the one hand, the Sage had knowledge of the truth of the quest, yet, on the other, would put hindrance in its way. The full articulation of the thought came not entirely home to Peregrine; he but scented the matter as it were from afar. The Sage's next words brought amazement to him.

"I know the woman you seek," he said briefly. There was no mistaking the assurance of the tone.

"You have seen her?" he cried, even as he had cried to Simon.

"Verily I have," returned Menippus. "Now listen. Pursuit of her is of little avail; that you have fully proved. I know her dwelling. She welcomes not all men to her presence. That you have had vision of her shows me that she desires yours. There is no need to question at the moment how this may be. We, who study the riddle of the Universe, know well that there are matters which lie beyond the comprehension of ordinary mortals. Doubtless you would find it hard to understand how I should have been aware of your presence in the snow-drift without making use of my physical faculties,—in this case the sight of my eyes. Nevertheless I did know, and to my knowledge is due the fact that you are now lying upon that couch. That is to us a simple matter, the A B C of our Science. In fact I doubt me that it goes beyond A. It is a mere question of vibration, to which the customarily accepted channels of communication are a hindrance rather than a help. You will discover this in the case of the blind. Deprived of the coarser physical attributes of sight, which read merely the heavy and slow vibrations, the mind is alert and attuned to the light and quick vibrations, which are, in a sense, of spirit rather than of matter. To make my meaning clearer,—one possessed of physical sight interprets rightly the vibrations received from an object before his eyes. This object emits heavy vibrations, which reach and correspond to the physical vibrations of the eye. Every object, whether near or far, whether hidden or actually apparent, emits vibrations, since all matter is alive. But,—and this I would have you note particularly,—that which is afar and hidden emits lighter vibrations, which cannot so readily be interpreted by a human being, who is, by reason of the possession of his physical senses, endowed with coarser vibrations. This is not always the case. There are those, who, in full possession of all their physical faculties, are yet able to receive, and at times interpret, the lightest vibrations in the Universe. But this is rare. You may take it as a general rule, that a blind man is more readily sensitive to hidden objects than one in possession of his sight, more readily aware of the presence of the quick and light vibrations of the spirit world. Again, a deaf man can receive the vibrations of sound from that same world, where one in possession of his hearing is dulled to them by reason of the presence of the coarser vibrations. This, no doubt, is strange to you, nevertheless it is a fact." He leaned back in his chair with a sigh, as of one who should say all this is mere child's play, yet it were well to give it to you.

"Candidly, I find it exceeding bewildering," said Peregrine.

"Under my tuition the bewilderment will pass," said Menippus indulgently. "I see you rarely endowed. You need but guidance and teaching in the matter. This I propose to give you."

Peregrine smiled somewhat grimly. "I doubt that you find in me an over-apt pupil," he returned. "Also, to what end may the teaching be? And how shall it lead me further on my quest, which I tell you very plainly I mean to pursue?"

Menippus pointed to the door.

"There," he said, "is your way out. You can leave me on the instant an' you will; pursue your quest your own way. You have proved whether it has so far been successful or no. If, on the other hand, you abide here with me, receive the instructions I will give you, I will lead you anon to the woman you seek. By yourself you will never find her; through me you will. You may see my words fairy-tale invention an' you choose. You have free choice in the matter. Think well on it." He turned calmly to his book, bending close over the pages. For aught of consideration he now gave Peregrine he might have been non-existent.

Peregrine lay still, gnawing his finger thoughtfully. Truly he did not particularly like the turn of matters. There was an unhealthy atmosphere about the close-draped apartment and the man's words which he found distasteful. An' the woman were indeed in existence he had rather trust to his own self to find her. Yet....

In this word he summed up the past year and more; saw himself weary, footsore, hungry, moreover sick at heart, and no nearer fulfilment of his quest, to all appearance, than at the outset. Here was definite promise of fulfilment. It was the unhealthiness of the man before him that displeased him. He saw the face of the woman clear-eyed, wonderful, as he had seen her on the first day of his vision, not as he had seen her as he lay in the snow. That he believed now to be but the distorted image of a fevered imagination. How should the woman he knew in his dreams have dealing with this old Sage? In one breath Peregrine found the notion unendurable; in the next, an' the Sage spoke truth, he saw here the only means of meeting with her. Yet did he speak truth? There was the crux of the whole question. Perchance it were wisdom to stay a while, and put the matter to the test. An' the promise were not proved, he could set out anew on his own account. In the meantime he must stay as pupil. This he found somewhat nauseating to his mind. His senses now more fully awake, he found the odour of the room strange, a curious mixture of burning herbs, incense, and with it the scent of accumulated dust. No breath of outside air reached his nostrils. The atmosphere was as unwholesome physically as his mental conception of it. Thus he vacillated between remaining and departing. Finally he made his choice. Truly it was made somewhat sulkily, and for lack of seeing a better one.

"I will remain," he said.

Menippus raised his head, looked at him as one bewildered.

"You spoke?" he asked.

"I said I would remain," returned Peregrine a trifle testily. When one has stated a difficult and reluctant decision, it is none too pleasant to be obliged to repeat the statement. It is in a manner lowering to one's dignity.

"You do well," returned Menippus calmly. "Yet I would have you bear in mind it is by your own free will that you remain."

"I am wholly aware of it," retorted Peregrine. This insistence on the matter displeased him.

"I will now," continued Menippus still calmly, "send for food. You must eat."

"I need food strangely little," quoth Peregrine, "seeing I have gone hungry the whole day, and, I judge, well into the night."

"I gave you a cordial when we carried you within," returned Menippus briefly. "There was food and drink in its strength." He went to the door and clapped his hands.

Into the room came Castrano, the negro, bearing on a tray dishes of various meats, and decanters of wine. He placed them on a table and withdrew. Peregrine got off the couch. He and Menippus ate together. He found the meal exceeding palatable. On its conclusion Menippus turned towards him.

"I will now show you the room where you will sleep," he said. He lead the way along a passage and to a door. Beyond it was a winding stair in a turret. Menippus entered the room with him; a small place it was, furnished with necessities and naught beyond.

"The place is at your full disposal," said Menippus. "I make you my guest in confidence. There is but one stipulation I would put to you. The winding stair beyond your chamber leads to precincts which are my concern alone. I pray you leave them unmounted. Since you are a man it is safe to make this request. An' you were a woman it would send you up them in haste at the first opportune moment."

"Humph!" said Peregrine, leaving the cynicism unanswered.

"And now I bid you good-night," said Menippus.

The Sage departed Peregrine sat down on his bed. By the light of a candle he surveyed the place. The walls were ochre-washed; the floor bare board, none too clean. Cobwebs hung about the ceiling; a waiting spider or two made dark blots on the soft grey nets. The bed was a straw mattress on wooden trestles, and covered by a somewhat mangey bearskin. A wooden chair, a rough oak chest, and a table made up the remainder of the furniture. Above the table was a slit of a window set far forward in a deep embrasure.

Peregrine crossed to the table, mounted it, and peered through the slit. The storm had spent itself. The world lay in still whiteness without. Overhead the sky was star-sprinkled, powdered with myriads of waking eyes. Peregrine felt strange comfort in their watchfulness.

CHAPTER XX

VIBRATIONS

TIME being the panacea for most ills as we are told, so we may well regard custom as the panacea for most distates. It is certain it proved a panacea for Peregrine's. Active dislike being presently dulled to indifference, interest anon awakened.

You cannot long remain in the company of an ardent believer without receiving some touch of his beliefs, be they in God, the Devil, or himself. Menippus believed in the two last, more particularly in himself, being fully persuaded that while the Devil lent him some little aid he could most readily have dispensed with his services altogether, have relied entirely upon his own power. Doubtless the Devil, his master, being most politic, endorsed this theory, the while he laughed in his sleeve.

Peregrine, exceeding open to influences, sucked up the mental atmosphere around him as a sponge sucks up water. He had no notion of his own tendency. An' he had, he might have been the better on his guard, though here a man's own skill is of little avail, he needs truly to put on the armour of light, as the Scriptures have it.

Being permeated, then, with the atmosphere, he lost his distaste, found interest awakening. This latter was small wonder: an' you had conquered dislike there is little doubt that attraction would follow. There was mystery enough in the Sage's doings to stir curiosity, marvel enough to carry one forward, and a certain matter-of-fact exactitude, withal, which threw any hint of pure charlatanism aside, forced reality to the front, even while it brought dread with it.

At the first he merely instilled certain teachings. Here are some of them.

"Vibration," he said, elaborating on the outline he had formerly given Peregrine, "is the first law to study. There is no single thing in the universe which does not emit vibrations,—matter, colour, light, and sound. To comprehend the whole riddle of life is but to attune oneself to the reception of these vibrations, and interpret them rightly. Like rushes to like. To make my meaning clearer, sound—the crash of a falling tree for example—emits vibrations to the ether. They travel across it till they reach some instrument attuned to receive them. Such is the normal human ear within a normal distance of the falling tree. The vibrations lessen in force the further they travel. Beyond a certain distance the physical ear is not sufficiently sensitive to receive them. But it is only on their reception by the instrument that the sound becomes interpreted in terms of fact. To an ear beyond the normal distance of sensing the vibrations, there would be no sound, because of the lack of its sensitiveness in receiving and recording them as they weaken. This would not prove their non-existence in the ether, but merely the defect in the instrument which might have received them. Have you followed me?"

Peregrine frowning somewhat, but not uninterested, made known that he had done so.

"Here," quoth Menippus, "I have dealt with the merely physical and actual. This same question of vibration extends to our reception of the vibrations of form, light, and colour by the eye; of the vibrations of scent by the nostrils; more grossly to our reception of the vibrations of form and quality by the touch. Leaving the more material, we will pursue the matter further, dwell for a moment on thought. The vibrations of thought, though quicker, lighter, and therefore less easy of reception by the heavy and material vibrations of ordinary mortals, are yet infinitely more powerful, infinitely more enduring than the vibrations from material objects. I give it as my experience that the vibrations of a thought, strongly sent forth, can endure throughout the centuries. Hence it is that certain sensitized minds can receive the vibrations of thoughts of bygone ages. These they believe to be their own, having made, to their knowledge, no study of them as the thoughts of others."

Here Peregrine, who had followed the argument closely enough, demurred. Having a brain of his own he now used it to some purpose.

"But," he argued shrewdly, "if, as you say, all new thought as men hold it, is but the vibration of thought of bygone centuries, where will you allow the beginning of thought? Presumably at one time it must have been new."

This one might have imagined a daunting question. To attempt to push it to a conclusion in accord with the views Menippus had just set forth would mean a staggering delving into infinite æons of time before which the finite brain might well reel.

Yet Menippus had his reply ready.

"All thought is but one expression of the Universal Mind, which has known no beginning, and will know no ending," he remarked gravely.

Peregrine was silent. He found himself neither sufficient theologian, philosopher, or scholar to gainsay this vast statement. In a sense he saw it might be truth, yet found it in a manner vaguely distorted by the mirror of speech in which it was reflected by Menippus. He ventured on another query.

"How an' the thought be evil?" he demanded.

"Rightly speaking," returned Menippus, "there is no evil. All vibration flows in harmony from the Universal Mind. The imperfect or wrongful reception of those vibrations by the material vibrations of man, sets up discord. This men term evil, and believe therefore that evil vibrations have flowed from without towards them, rather than recognizing that the fault lies in themselves. Those who attune themselves rightly can receive the whole stored up thought and knowledge of the centuries. This is wisdom, and wisdom is power."

Here was the mere jargon of his trade. It is true there were some who believed this doctrine they preached. Excellent sounding, and none too easily refuted, it had deceived more questioners than Peregrine. Yet it is very certain that Menippus, though he had it ready enough on his tongue, held it not in his mind. Frankly, he saw two powers in the universe, or better speaking three, since I have shown you in what estimation he held his own. An' the matter be put plainly, he had sought to make the other two subservient to his. This, in the one case, meant deliberate warfare, finally sheer ignoring; in the other, he saw himself victor and master, recognized not at all that he was slave.

Here was the beginning of his teaching. Later he led him further, gave him in outline some inkling of the founding of the Order of Lux. For what it is worth I set it forth here.

The Order, so said Menippus, was of great antiquity. It was founded by three Egyptian Seers, psychics of much power. For the space of nine moons they had sojourned in the desert, food and water being brought to them by messengers. They spoke to none save each other. Now at the ninth month, at the full of the moon, they saw the Sign of the Triangle in the Heavens, and the three stood in a circle, making the Sign of the Triangle each with his own hand and that of his neighbour, thumb to thumb, and forefinger to forefinger. And the names of the three who did this were Pharos, Zadkiel, and Ramah. And above the Triangle they saw the Lotus Flower, and above the Lotus Flower the Sign of Triple Power; while the whole was backgrounded by the Sign of the Rising Sun, though it was yet moonlight when they looked on these signs. And they heard, so says the legend, a Voice speaking to the three, which bade them return to the Inner Temple, and in seven weeks the seven rules of the novitiate should be made known to them, for each week a rule. And in seven months should the seven rules of the brotherhood be made known to them, for each month a rule. And in seven years should the seven rules of the priesthood be made known to them, for each year a rule. Thus in seven years, seven months, and seven weeks from the first seeing of the Sign, was the Order of Lux perfected. And the three cast lots as to who should be chiefest among them, for they were all three of a royal house. The lot fell upon Zadkiel.

Then he entered into the silence for seven days, and the seven rules of the High Priest were made known to him, for each day a rule. Now, none but the High Priest and one other know these seven rules: the High Priest tells them to his successor. But lest there should fall mischance of the death of both, and for fear lest the rules be lost, they have been written, and placed in a casket kept in the innermost Sanctuary of the Temple, and the High Priest alone possesses the key of this casket.

Now here is a further matter which is somewhat strange. Though the Order is the Order of Lux, and its chief symbol is the Rising Sun, the Temple where the casket lay was the Temple of the Moon, in the plains of furthest Egypt. Here the Moon Ritual was performed by the Ancients each month.

All this Menippus told Peregrine. Further, he told him that one night at the full of the moon he should see the ritual as it was performed by those ancient priests, and, moreover, see the priests themselves. At this you may well believe Peregrine found himself somewhat incredulous; but it is certain that later his incredulity was shaken.

CHAPTER XXI

MOON RITUAL

THIS chapter may well be omitted by the incredulous. For my part I know not fully whether to see in it mere hypnotic influence, or some power more evil. Possibly both had dealing in the matter. As it occurred, I will give it you, as briefly as may be, since I have little liking for these doings.

One night, the moon being very clear and full, Peregrine was roused from slumber by a rap on his chamber door. Opening it he saw Castrano the negro without, bearing a lantern in his hand.

"My master, Menippus, bids you follow me, an' you would see that which will chance in the Temple this night," he said shortly.

Donning his clothes anew, and wrapping his cloak around him, Peregrine prepared to follow the negro. The latter led the way in silence to the hall, and thence down vaulted passages which struck with a strange chillness. From the manner of their descent Peregrine perceived that they led underground, penetrating deep into the earth. They were hewn out of rock and stone, very rough and jagged. Far above him was their arched roof plastered in some manner.

After walking five minutes or so, Castrano came to a halt opposite a great door, nail-studded. This he opened, and in the dim light Peregrine saw steps descending. Castrano led the way down them; signed to Peregrine to take his place by a pillar, indicated a stone seat, whispered an injunction to remain where he found himself, and so left him.

Peregrine's eyes becoming accustomed to the gloom, he looked around him. It was a dark vaulted place, very lofty. In each of the four corners, barely discernible through the darkness, were huge marble statues. To the left was an arch containing seven hanging lamps, their dim flame casting a faint light upon a dark object below it. What this object was Peregrine knew not. It appeared to be a cabinet of black wood.

In the middle of the Temple was a stone pillar some three and a half feet in height, the base pentagnol, the capital slightly hollowed. Smoke ascended from it in a misty blue column. The burning substance upon it gave forth a strange heavy scent. Above it hung a lamp half hidden by the ascending smoke. Around the pillar, on the black marble floor, was drawn a great circle in white chalk. An outer circle surrounded the floor of the whole Temple. This Peregrine saw but faintly, and only as he peered from right to left, marking all that reached his eye.

His gaze coming back again to the pillar, he saw Menippus standing near it, within the inner circle. He had not marked him previously, and believed this to be his first appearance. He was standing motionless and rigid, robed in purple, white, and scarlet; Peregrine felt his eyes drawn to him by some impelling force.

For a space Menippus remained thus; then Peregrine saw him slowly stretch out his arms. Through the Temple came his whispered voice, gradually gathering in force.

"*Adonay! Adonay! Adonay!*"

came the cry. And then again louder.

"*Adonay! Adonay! Adonay!*"

It seemed to Peregrine that the atmosphere around him trembled, as the cry came floating through the Temple. And then it came a third time.

"*Adonay! Adonay! Adonay!*"

Now it penetrated to the furthest corners, echoed hollowly in the vaulted roof. He was very sure that the air shook.

Still the cry went on, and with it further words. They were uttered in Latin. For your better understanding of the ritual I give you the translation. The utterance of the words came in curious waves of sound, rising, falling, beating through space; collecting, so it seemed, power and force, in their inexorable rhythm.

"*Adonay! Adonay! Adonay!*

Thou that dwellest in the spaceless void,

Adonay! Adonay! Adonay!

Thou that dwellest in the illimitable silence,

Adonay! Adonay! Adonay!

Bring to us thine aid."

The voice fell to silence; a breath of wind swept through the Temple.

"*Adonay! Adonay! Adonay!*

Indomitable Ruler of the Firmaments,

Adonay! Adonay! Adonay!

Invisible Wanderer of the trackless stars,

Adonay! Adonay! Adonay!

Lend to us thy power."

Again the wind swept through the Temple, falling once more to a deathly stillness. Small points of light focussed, broke, and scattered through the gloom.

"*Adonay! Adonay! Adonay!*

Majestic Creator of the Vast All,

Adonay! Adonay! Adonay!

Breath of the Boundless Universe,

Adonay! Adonay! Adonay!

Give to us creation and the breath of life."

And then, lastly, the supreme utterance given with the whole collective force of will:

"*Messias Soter Emanuel Sabaoth Adonay, te adore et invoco.*"

Now the wind swept through the Temple in a volume, swaying the lamps till their chains jangled, beating down the smoke from the pillar till it spread in clouds around it. Again the stillness fell. The air around the pillar cleared.

Now Peregrine saw four figures standing by it, where previously there had been but one,—men robed in purple, white, and scarlet, as Menippus was robed; and round the forehead of each was a gold fillet fronted by the Rising Sun. From whence they had made their appearance he knew not, but it is very certain that the awe brought to his heart by the sweeping wind remained with it in their presence. The still air felt almost ice cold. Peregrine shivered, and drew his cloak closer around him the while he gazed, his eyes rivetted upon the pillar and the four figures. While fully aware of their actual presence, he was yet imbued with a sense of unreality, and more especially a sensation of unsafety. He felt somewhat as a man might feel, who sees poisoned arrows falling round him, and knows himself vulnerable at every point. An' he be not wounded, it will be by some good chance, rather than by any protection he can afford himself.

Then he saw that another light had entered the Temple,—pale moonlight falling straight upon the circle where the four stood, though from whence it entered he knew not. Now he heard chanting coming from the four; saw some ceremony was in progress. This was none too easy for the uninitiated to follow.

At the first they stood, arms wide-spread, rhythmic syllables falling from their lips in measured tone, with curious undulation and dwelling on the vowels. It seemed, indeed, naught but vowels that they uttered with the wailing cry as of some Banshee. Next, the cry dying away, they bowed themselves in silence to the earth, touching the black marble floor with their fillet-bound foreheads. Then, standing again upright, the figure nearest him went up to the pillar, took from it with a pair of golden tongs, what appeared to be glowing charcoal. This he placed in a gold censer. Standing, then, beside the pillar, Menippus, who faced him, came towards him, blew upon the charcoal till it glowed to deeper crimson. Half unconsciously, through the ritual, Peregrine found his brain recording sentences. Here was the first.

"And the Wind of the North shall blow upon the Fire of the South that it increase in fervour, since from the South cometh the Purifying Fire."

Menippus moved back to his place, and the figure to his right came forward. This one scattered drops of water on the pillar, which hissed as they fell among the burning mass. Next Menippus came down, breathed upon the vessel the figure held.

"And the Wind of the North shall blow upon the Waters of the East, that they quench not the Fires of the South."

Here the figure holding the vessel of water carried it to him with the censer. Thrusting his hand into the vessel he scattered drops upon the charcoal in the censer. Again there was a sound of hissing; but the smoke from the censer continued to ascend. He stepped back, and Menippus came forward, signing symbols over the water, finally scattering drops around the pillar and upon the other three.

"And the Wind of the North scatters the Waters of the East, purifying those on whom the drops shall fall."

Now he again returned to his place, and the figure to his left came forward. From a bag of purple stuff he drew forth grain, threw it on the pillar where it was caught by the fire, and flame sprung up. Once more Menippus came forward. Here he took grain from the hands of the figure who held the bag, carried it to the figure bearing the censer, threw grain on the censer.

"And the Wind of the North shall carry the offering of the West, that it be purified by the Fires of the South."

All four now returning to their former places, again the wailing chant rang through the Temple with ever increasing insistence. The vibratory strength of the ascending and descending cry brought back to Peregrine's mind somewhat of the Sage's teaching. He perceived in it new meaning, felt, in a measure, the vibrations correspond with other subtle vibrations in the atmosphere around him. Together they formed a strange harmony. Now he saw Menippus stand with arms again outstretched, saw the figures South, West, and East, scatter burning charcoal, grain, and water upon the ground, found his brain again recording words, even though they were not heard in actual sense by his ears.

"Thus purified upon the altar, further purified by the breath of the Wind from the North, we return these gifts to the Earth, in the Name of the Great Lord Adonay, Creator of the Universe, Lord of the World, Ruler of all Creation, of the Elements, of things animate and inanimate. Adonay! Adonay! Adonay!"

Now they moved in measured tread around the pillar, chanting as they went. Nine times they circled it, coming at length to a stand in their former position. The chanting now held a tone of praise rather than of invocation. Words after this fashion came to his mind:

"Light of the Sleeping World,

Globe suspended in Boundless Space,

Watcher of the Silence,

We worship Thee.

"In the ninth month of Thy Reign,

In the time of Plenteousness,

In the time of Harvest,

We worship Thee.

"Looking upon the Fruitful Earth,

Looking upon the Bounteous Plenitude,

Looking upon the Gifts of Nature,

We worship Thee.

"Thy light is falling on the Ripened Harvest,

Thy light is falling on the Whitened Cornfields,
Thy light is falling on the Purple Vineyards.
We worship Thee.

"For the white Oil of Gladness,
For the golden Corn of Strength,
For the red Wine of Sweetness,
We worship Thee.

"O Golden Sphere,
We worship Thee.
O Queen of Night,
We worship Thee."

He saw that the moonlight was shifting. It no longer fell full upon the circle. The chanting came with a tone of finality. He received now no sense of words, knew merely that the ritual was drawing to an end.

On a sudden the chant ceased. An extraordinary silence fell upon the Temple. At the same instant he saw that the three figures had disappeared. Menippus alone stood rigid by the pillar. Peregrine found himself trembling. A slight sound drew his eyes to the dark object before the archway. A face, white and frightened, was peering from it. Peregrine made a quick step forward. On the instant his arm was seized. Turning he saw Castrano.

"It is ended," whispered the negro, and hurried him from the Temple.

CHAPTER XXII

DEVIL WORSHIP

PEREGRINE found his interest fired by these matters that I have shown you. Menippus giving solid proof of his power, he doubted not that eventually at his will he could make good his word, bring him in contact with the woman he sought; though, to speak truth, his desire for the meeting had somewhat lessened. There was enough here to absorb his mind. Subtle flattery led him to belief in his own power. He saw himself presently a rival of his teacher, his equal if not his master in the possession of knowledge.

This led him to desire quicker advancement than Menippus was willing to allow. He knew full well there were at times mystic ceremonies in progress at which his presence was not requested. They were held in the Temple. This he learned by midnight prowling. Soft-footed he had slipped more than once from his chamber. The guidance of a murmuring voice had led him to the Temple door. Courage was not strong enough to bring him to an entry; his ear pressed against the door he had listened. Here and there he caught a Latin word, isolated enough to bring him no inkling of the context. Curiosity fell hot upon him. He had made scrupulous avoidance of the turret stair. Menippus having put a request in that matter, honour as a guest bound him to its observance. Here he felt no such qualm; it was merely that he lacked courage to turn the handle of the door. An' he could gain knowledge of what passed within, without Menippus being aware of his entry, he would do so.

He set himself to think. Observance showed him, that on such nights as the murmuring voice proceeded from the Temple, Menippus first made visit to the precincts beyond the turret stair, moreover marked that when he descended again he was not alone. This brought him to a conclusion. In the future he sought not his couch before midnight: ear alert he awaited the Sage's ascent of the stair.

Six nights he waited to no purpose. Judging the passing of time by the march of the moon across the sky, he relaxed his visit when she was over, or near, a yew tree without. He made allowance each night for her later rising. Clear skies favoured this reckoning. The seventh night, patience being by now well-nigh exhausted, and sleep lying heavy on his eyelids, he heard a footfall without, marked its ascent of the turret stair. Here was his opportunity. He slipped softly from his chamber, and adown the corridor.

He had time enough for his purpose. Never less than twenty minutes or so had elapsed betwixt the Sage's ascent and descent of the stair. He passed down the corridor, made his way to the dimly lighted hall, and thence to the vaulted passages leading to the Temple. The silence was profound: here in the passages darkness reigned. He groped his way along them, feeling to the left for the Temple door, as he had felt more than once already. Anon his fingers touched it. Excitement beating high in his heart, he found the handle, turned it softly. The door did not yield to his pressure. Bringing his shoulder to bear against it, he found it locked. Here, at the moment he believed his purpose accomplished, defeat faced him. An' he had not waited seven nights for this moment the disappointment had been less hard to endure. Now he felt it very bitterly.

Casting about in his mind what next course to pursue, he saw on a sudden from afar whence he had come, a swaying light. A dim speck at the first, it grew larger. There was small doubt but that it came from a lamp carried by one approaching the place where he was standing. To remain where he was were madness. Turning, he groped swiftly down the passage away from the light.

Some twenty paces or so further he found the wall come to an end. Feeling cautiously he found the passage turn leftwards. An' the bearer of the light stopped at the Temple door, this gave him cover. He paused to listen, ready to make further flight should the steps come near him. He heard them echoing softly in the vaulted spaces; anon they came to a halt. He fetched a deep breath of relief. He heard the turning of a key.

Waiting to be sure of safety, he saw on a sudden a gleam of light above him, perceived that it came from a square opening in the wall. His brain worked quickly. Someone within the Temple had lighted a lamp or candles. Here was a wall of the Temple, and a window giving on to it. An' he could gain the window, chance had brought him a safer means of viewing the ceremony about to take place than had he ventured through the door. Also he saw no means whereby he could now enter undiscovered. Had he guessed at the truth of the happening, he would have known that Castrano had forgotten to make the place ready; had come swiftly to repair the omission, and return to his couch before Menippus arrived at the Temple. Even now Castrano was leaving it, and Peregrine would have found entrance easy; though for exit later I am none so sure.

Peregrine felt the wall below the window. The stones, rough and jutting forward in places, would afford him slight foothold. He set himself to climb. Grazing knee and hand somewhat, and with danger of a fall, he gained the aperture above him. It was a square opening, barred, giving on to the Temple within; sufficiently deep, too, to afford him seating of some sort. He saw clearly the risk of Menippus glancing towards it, perceiving his crouching figure. This risk he was ready to take. There is naught to be gained without some venture. Getting his seat secure, and holding to the bars, he looked within. The place was as he had seen it on the night of his entry there, save that, instead of the stone pillar in the middle of the floor, there was now an altar against the wall to his right. Peregrine guessed some new ritual about to be performed.

No one was in sight. Whoever had lighted the candles on the altar had now withdrawn. Peregrine debated for a moment, had idea of making descent, of trying again the Temple door. This thought he put aside for two reasons. First, he ran grave risk of coming upon Menippus; second, he saw himself vastly safer without the Temple than within it. He drew his cloak close around him, trusting to its darkness to give appearance of shadow in the embrasure, and waited.

He had not long to wait. The door opened: through the gloom Peregrine saw two figures enter, one small, in size no more than a child. He heard the lock turned behind them. An' he had possessed courage sufficient to try the door formerly, it would have availed him little.

The figures descended the steps, came forward towards the light. Now Peregrine saw them plainly, a small boy dressed as an acolyte, and swinging a golden censer; behind him Menippus vested as a priest. They came before the altar. Then Menippus began to speak. Familiar words struck on Peregrine's ear, setting his heart thumping. He heard the boy's voice come in with response,—a lifeless voice, as of one drugged.

Heart and brain sick, he crouched rigid. Here was horror of which he had never dreamt. But for the bars, he had made an entry at whatever danger to life and limb, stopped the horrid sacrilege. He could not look at it. Slithering from the wall, bruising himself in the descent, he gained the passage, made along it, and thence to his own chamber. Here he found his breath coming in deep sobs.

"I had not known," he said; and sank upon his knees.

Shuddering he knelt there, knowing nothing of the passing of time. Horror had beaten upon his soul: his body was numbed. This was where his quest had brought him. Dazed and sick he found his strength spent.

Steps passing his door brought him to himself. Wit in a measure returned, he saw that flight must be his with no delay. Then another thing struck him. He thought of the child he had seen. What an' he had been trapped to this pass? Peregrine saw not his own flight without some assurance on this score. To leave the child were sheer cowardice.

He waited; presently heard Menippus descend. A moment or so later the place lay in dead silence. Peregrine made for the door. No thought of honour held him now. He had his foot upon the turret stair, was up it in soft bounds. Atop he came upon a door, a staple pushed across it. To pull it back was but an instant's work; the next, he had entered the chamber.

The moonlight fell across the floor, and upon a couch. On the couch lay a boy, a small thin child. He started up on the sound of the opening door, turned a pitiful face, and great dark eyes towards it.

"Yes?" he queried, alert, ready for bidding. Then on a sudden he shrank. "Who is it?" he asked fearfully.

"Hush!" whispered Peregrine.

"Ah, who is it?" pleaded the child frightened. "I am blind."

The pathetic utterance smote straight to Peregrine's heart.

"You poor little misery!" he ejaculated on a note of tenderness. "See here, listen well. I wish you no ill, naught but good. Bide you willingly here?"

The boy fell to trembling. "Willingly? Ah, no!"

"Was what you did this night willing service on your part?" asked Peregrine, striving to keep severity from his voice.

"I know not what I did," replied the boy. "I act as he bids me; I say words which he has taught me. Knowing not their meaning yet I dread to say them."

"That," said Peregrine very low, "is well. Will you trust yourself to me?"

"Sir," replied the child, "I know not who you are. But, an' your heart is like to your voice, I trust you very freely."

Peregrine smiled grimly. "We'll leave my heart out of the question," he said. "Truly it, or my own foolishness, has brought me to a pretty pass. Would you leave this place an' you could?"

The boy started from the couch.

"You will take me from it! Ah, sir, sir!" Groping towards Peregrine he found his hand. Down on his knees he fell to kissing it with fervour.

Peregrine hauled him to his feet.

"Save your gratitude till the matter is accomplished," quoth he. "We have first to make our way from the place."

This brought the child to his senses. "I know not how that may be done," he faltered. "Castrano sleeps across the hall door. I have heard him snore as we passed the hall from the Temple. There is no other way out."

"Then we must make a way," said Peregrine very cheerfully. "And first you must put on some clothes."

He found doublet, breeches, and hose lying on a chair; aided the boy with their donning. The child clad himself, ear alert, fearful of his own breathing. Long imprisonment he had borne with resignation: hope bringing life to his heart quickened it also to fear of hope frustrated.

The boy garbed, the two slipped softly down the turret stair, careful of each footfall. Thence they gained Peregrine's chamber. Here he made the bolt fast: this gave him, he felt, breathing space.

"Since no exit can be made by the door," he remarked, "we must e'en make it by the window. 'Tis somewhat narrow, but I have had my head through it more than once; and where a man's head can pass, his body can certainly follow. You, I think, can go through it with ease."

Crossing to the bed he pulled a rough woollen blanket from below the bearskin. With the aid of a knife he proceeded to tear it into strips. These he knotted firmly. Mounting the table, he threw one end from the window measuring its length.

"'Tis somewhat short," he said peering downwards, "and 'twill mean a drop, but with luck no bones need be broken. First I will lower you, then make descent myself."

He hauled up the improvised rope. Making one end fast to the table, he knotted the other under the boy's arms.

"When I come down above you," he said, "I must needs cut the rope below me, and let you fall. Get to your feet on the instant, and go some paces away, that I fall not on the top of you."

He helped the boy to the table, put him through the window.

"You must trust me," said Peregrine kindly.

"Oh, I do!" replied the boy fervently.

"Keep off the wall with your feet, an' you can," said Peregrine, and began to lower.

The rope paid out to its fullest, Peregrine got to the window himself. On the ledge he dragged the table upwards, wedged it across the narrow opening.

"Pray Heaven the rope bears us both," he muttered. "There was no other way."

Feet braced against the wall he began the descent. To the child below it appeared an eternity before Peregrine's foot touched his shoulder.

"Ha!" said Peregrine. "Now prepare to drop."

Swinging by one arm he felt for the rope by his knees, and hacked. A moment's work, and it gave. The boy rolled on the grass below, none the worse save for a slight jarring.

"All well," he whispered, scrambling away from the wall. Now Peregrine dropped lightly; was up in a moment but little shaken. He looked at the hanging rope.

"Leaving traces of our flight behind us, we depart," he said grimly.

Taking the boy by the arm he made swift way across the grass, out of the moonlight, into cover of an adjoining wood.

CHAPTER XXIII

ABBOT HILARY

ABBOT HILARY came riding through Thorn Wood when the morning was yet young. Matters ecclesiastic having taken him from Dieuporte three days previously, he was now returning to it. Going leisurely enough, conning his breviary as he rode, he found time to sniff the good morning air, mark the chequered lights and shadows on the moss and on the tree trunks.

A portly man this Abbot, shrewd-eyed and kindly. Big-voiced, you heard his tones quaking an' they thundered forth reproof: solemn in absolution, you heard them like a deep-toned bell guiding you to harbourage from storm. With a heart as big as his voice, he loved mankind hugely; found excuse for the sinner even while he denounced the sin. His brain, alert within his massive head, was quick to detect lying and fraud. This he hated very deeply, as generous men hate such dealings. He loved the open air and God's sunshine, his mind as healthy as his robust body.

Riding now leisurely enough, muttering Latin psalm the while he rode, his eye roving now and again from the open page of his breviary to the dappled sunlight around him, he checked his horse on a sudden, bringing the Latin phrase on his tongue to a like halt.

At the foot of a tree he saw a white-faced boy stretched upon the ground. His attitude showed exhaustion; the whiteness of his face faintness possibly akin to death.

Abbot Hilary was off his horse in a trice, despite the somewhat unwieldiness of his size. Hitching the bridle to a crooked branch of a tree he made over to the boy, came down on his knees beside him. Slipping his fingers beneath the doublet he satisfied himself that life was not extinct, and thereupon fell to chafing the child's hands. A crackling in the bushes behind him stayed this business for a moment, brought his head round to see who was approaching.

From out the trees came a tall man garbed in motley, bearing a broad leaf carefully in his hands. On seeing the figure by the boy, Peregrine came quickly forward. Heeding the bearing of the leaf less well the water it contained trickled from it to the ground.

"Let the child be!" cried Peregrine very sternly.

The Abbot got to his feet, faced him, a big man astounded.

"Truly," he said on a tone conciliatory, "I meant the boy no ill. Seeing him lying there fainting and alone, I but sought to restore him to consciousness."

"I crave your pardon," said Peregrine quickly, very apologetic, "I thought 'twas another knelt beside him: one with whose company we may very well dispense." He looked now ruefully at his leaf. "And like a fool I've spilled the water," he remarked.

"You fetched it from the stream yonder," said the Abbot, knowing Thorn Wood well, every inch on it. "Methinks 'twere simpler matter to carry the child to the stream than bring the stream to the child. In the first case we can be more lavish with our restorative."

Peregrine laughed. "You speak very truly," quoth he.

The Abbot picked up the fainting boy from the ground, lifting him as though he lifted a mere featherweight, and straightway made off in strides among the trees, Peregrine following in his wake.

Down by the water,—a narrow silver stream flowing among ferns and mosses,—they laved the boy's temples and wrists, got drops between his lips. Anon he came to himself, sat up somewhat feebly.

"I will come on the instant," he cried faintly, his mind back at the place he had left.

"Tut, tut," spoke Peregrine soothingly, "never trouble yourself, child. There's no more coming and going for you at that scoundrel's bidding."

"Ah, I forgot," cried the boy fetching a deep breath of relief. "Who else is here?" he asked on a sudden.

"Rightly speaking," said Peregrine smiling at the Abbot, "I know not myself. But assuredly 'tis one who has befriended you very well."

The Abbot laughed, big-voiced and hearty. "I am one Hilary at your service, Abbot of Dieuporte," said he. "Methinks 'twere well you both accompanied me thither, that this child may there gain rest from evident over-fatigue."

This proposal fell well enough on Peregrine's ears as far as it concerned the boy. For his own part he had yet further to travel, though he was willing enough to accompany them to the place, wherever it might chance to be. Keeping his own plans silent for the moment, however, he acceded readily enough to the Abbot's suggestion. Picking up the boy again, the Abbot led the way back to his horse.

"Do you mount," said he to Peregrine, "and take the lad before you. Methinks you, too, have done walking enough for the present."

Here Peregrine demurred somewhat, being loth to take such summary possession of the other's horse; but the Abbot pressed his point. Presently mounted they moved on at walking pace among the trees. Lulled by the movement the boy fell asleep, lying snug in Peregrine's arms.

"An' it be not impertinence," said the Abbot, "might I ask whither you two were faring when I chanced on you?"

"'Tis no impertinence," laughed Peregrine, "yet it is a question to which I can find no answer, since truly I knew not myself."

"Hmm!" mused the Abbot, drawing down his eyebrows.

Peregrine, seeing the boy sleeping, now began to talk more openly.

"This child," said he, "has been in the possession of a very evil scoundrel. It is true that I have been heartily gulled by him myself. Now I know him in his true colours, which are certainly very black and filthy. Two nights agone we made our escape from him; since, we have wandered the woods, eating blackberries to stay our hunger. I can fend well enough for myself. For the boy it is another matter. Therefore I see very clearly that Providence sent you in our path."

"Truly," said the Abbot, "I see His guidance in all ways."

"I do not," returned Peregrine very frankly. "But then it is not probable that you have followed paths like to those I have traversed."

The Abbot smiled, humorous, though grave. "I meant I saw His guidance in the paths He bids us follow. An' stiff necked we follow those of our own choosing, methinks 'tis the Devil leads the way."

Peregrine rubbed his chin. "There I am with you very freely. But how about this child? He found himself in paths where truly I can see none of God's guidance, and would hesitate to say I saw the Devil's leading, since assuredly the path was no choice of the boy's."

Abbot Hilary mused, looking down among the trees. "God has His Own methods," he said presently. "At times He leads by strange paths, which, were they of our own choosing, would soil us sadly; but, since for some hidden purpose of His Own He takes us by them, He leads us through the mire undefiled."

Peregrine nodded quick assent. "Here you have given clear tongue to the matter. The child that lies in my arms has been present with evil, yet he is not evil. Unwittingly he has taken part in the worst sacrilege, yet he is no sacrilegist. Thus much I have learned from him. How he came to such straights he knows not. He has no memory for aught but the place from which I brought him. An' you can gain full speech from him as he gave it to me, and cleanse his mind from memory of past foulness, 'twill be well for his soul."

For a few moments the Abbot made no answer. Then he said quietly, "What do you propose for the boy?"

"That he remain with you," returned Peregrine on the instant. "In the first place, I am no fit company for him; in the second place, he is blind and needs safe harbourage; in the third place, he should learn forgetfulness of the past, which you can teach him."

"And how for yourself?" replied the Abbot smiling.

Peregrine's face fell to rigid lines.

"For myself, I have a quest before me; perchance a goal to reach. Twice I have been deluded, put off the track. It may be death will overtake me e'er the quest be fulfilled. That must be as will be. I only know I must pursue it."

The Abbot was silent a while, his eyes bent upon the ground. Methinks, by the movement of his lips, he uttered some inward prayer. Anon he spoke kindly.

"You spoke of a goal perchance to be reached. How know you that same goal lies not at Dieuporte? For my part I have a very fair inkling that it is so."

Peregrine shook his head. "You may be right, but I do not think it is. Yet, an' you will take the boy, you will be doing a goodly deed."

"That I will do readily enough," replied the Abbot gravely.

Here a silence fell. And so they pursued their way among the trees. Great beech trees they were; the trunks grey and purple, flecked with green and silver; the leaves russet and brown, toned by the touch of autumn. Long shaded glades stretched on either hand. Now and again a rabbit scuttled down one of them. Small stirrings among the undergrowth bespoke the presence of dormice, squirrels, and other woodland creatures. The silence was occasionally broken by the harsh note of a pheasant.

Anon ascending somewhat, and the trees thinning, they had glimpse between them of a valley beyond lying in autumn sunlight. Here there were more woods, blue in the hazy distance. Coming from among the trees, Peregrine had sight of grey towers in the valley; judged, and rightly, it was Dieuporte lying in its peaceful shelter. Now they began to descend. The way led adown a lane bordered on either hand by blackberry bushes laden with dark luscious fruit. At the bottom a stream crossed it, stepping stones affording traverse for foot passengers. Now the road widened, lying between sedgy meadows, where cows stood in the shadow of the willows. After a mile or so it turned leftwards, and here Dieuporte lay straight before them.

The sight of its grey towers stirred Peregrine strangely. For a moment he found himself ready to believe the Abbot's words, to see his goal within the quiet place. Now I know not precisely why he put the thought aside; but, methinks that being twice deluded by the words of men, he had no mind to find himself deluded a third time; thought rather to trust to his own self in the matter. Yet, for all that, the sight of the place moved him strangely, as I have said. He felt like a man travelling in very barbarous lands come within sight of a home. And further, felt that within that home dwelt one long desired, long needed, yet never attained. Some mighty power seemed to draw him to it even while his spirit rebelled.

Telling himself imagination and illusion were present with him, he set himself to combat it. Had not bitterness from past disappointment been present with him, perchance he might have read some omen in the still hush of the autumn air, have found in it a tenseness as of expectant waiting. The red-dyed leaves hung motionless on the trees above him as he rode, rusty, stained as though with blood. The combat within his soul was sharp and fierce. His own will gained the mastery. He strangled the thought, flung it aside as rank sentiment. A little breeze passed around him, stirring the leaves on the trees. It came like a breath of regret. Perchance Abbot Hilary recognized it unwittingly, for he sighed.

The boy moved in Peregrine's arms, yawned, and presently awakened.

"Where are we?" he asked.

"At a place where you will be in safety and well tended," returned Peregrine.

"You will be with me?" asked the child very anxious. And the Abbot waited for the answer.

"Nay," responded Peregrine. "I have further to travel. But you need have no fear. An' I were not assured of your welfare I would not leave you. You will bide here."

There was finality in the words which the child did not gainsay. Too long had command been known to him for him to be unwitting of its tone. Peregrine felt him tremble in his arms, but no word came from his lips.

The Abbot knocked upon the Mercy Door. It opened, showing a lay brother standing within.

"Take the horse," said the Abbot to him after a word of greeting.

The brother departed with it, the Abbot turned to Peregrine.

"You are determined to continue your journey?"

"I am determined," replied Peregrine briefly.

"Ah, well," returned the Abbot cheerfully, "God's times are not always as ours. You will at least wait till I send food to you here. You have fasted long enough, methinks. Blackberries make but poor sustenance. You may rest assured of the boy's welfare. You did good service when you rescued him. Farewell, my son, and God speed you on your quest." He paused a moment, looked at him very searchingly. "An' I were to prophesy," he said smiling, "I should tell of your coming to your goal e'er long. Fare you well." He passed across the courtyard, his hand on the child's shoulder.

Anon, with a well-filled wallet, Peregrine turned his back on Dieuporte, made his way adown the valley.

CHAPTER XXIV

AT DIEUPORTE

E'ER we follow Peregrine in his further wanderings, it were well, methinks, to remain a brief space at Dieuporte. To leave on the instant the child committed by him to Abbot Hilary's care, were to my mind to leave him somewhat summarily. An' you are of my way of thinking, have found interest in the boy, you would know something of his further welfare. Having brought him to harbourage, it is restful to dwell a short time with him.

You may be sure the child found the Abbey restful. In the first place, it held a rare atmosphere of sanity and homeliness. Herein it differed from the dwelling he had left as greatly as good wheaten bread differs from tainted dishes. In the second place, he experienced safety in the presence of the big Abbot and his colleagues. This he felt without fully realizing that he did so. His mind, hitherto tensioned to an unwholesome strain by the very evil will of Menippus, now found entire relaxation. He slept, ate, and slept again, his strength vastly recuperating thereby.

He spent long hours in the sunny garden, mainly in company with young Brother Francis, to whose charge the Abbot had specially allotted him. Here, in spite of his blindness, he became aware of the beauty around him. He felt the soft wind, heard its rustling in the trees; heard also the low notes of the wood pigeons; smelt the sweet scent of the flowers. In the quiet orderliness of the place, its stateliness, yet its simplicity and its homely happiness, his rightful heritage of childhood, long denied him, came to birth. He lost his furtive look, ceased to start at sudden sounds; his peaked face grew to plumpness, a delicate colour tinged his cheeks. Anon, he was heard to laugh. This sound pleased Brother Francis vastly, and the Abbot no less.

Having good care for his body, they forgot not his soul. There was no proof he was a Christian. Having been in the charge of Menippus from babyhood the Abbot saw the matter more than doubtful. Gentle questioning of the child led him to pretty full knowledge of the manner of place from which Peregrine had rescued him, and the corruption in it. Of the truths of Christianity he was entirely ignorant. Here the Abbot took instruction upon himself. This required careful handling, since to bring knowledge of truth home to him was at the same time to show him more fully the evil by which he had been surrounded. What Menippus had taught most foully must now be taught in its full beauty. Briefly, to bring him to the sunlight were at the same time to make him aware of the darkness of the pit he had left.

Figuratively speaking we see the Abbot holding him in strong arms while he looked backward on the horror. The tears that came at the knowledge of it Abbot Hilary dried; the shuddering he stilled. He told him an ancient history. This was the story of the Three Holy Children cast into a fiery furnace. He told him they had walked the flames unscathed, since One was with them; their garments,—even the hair upon their heads,— escaping the smallest scent of fire. From it he drew a moral bearing on the boy's own case. The child listened wondering, and greatly comforted. The horror of uncleanness fell somewhat from him at the tale. Also, for his further comfort, the Abbot told him of Baptism, and Forgiveness for past wrong.

The boy drank in his teaching eagerly. The very sensitiveness of his mind, which Menippus had used for his own ends, made him the more open to present influence. Body and soul, he expanded, like a bud in the sunlight; it needed but the seal of pardon, like the kiss of the sun at noontide, to bring his soul to full flower.

He knew himself by no name. Menippus had given him none. "Boy" was sufficient for his needs. It had been, "Boy, come hither; Boy, do this." Now known more tenderly as "Child" it were yet well that the presently Christian should have a Christian name.

Here Brother Francis arraigned the saints before him for his selection, gave him their history in brief. This was pleasant enough occupation. To sit on an old stone seat in the garden, to hear the humming of the bees among the flowers mingling with the musical voice of Brother Francis, was a joy to the small selector. He lent grave ear to the telling. Coming to St. Michael he embraced him readily. Here was warrior enough to delight his heart. He saw himself well protected in the future. An' the Saint himself had other matters on hand, what simpler than that he should order a deputy to take charge? This thought he made naïvely known, thereby causing Brother Francis to smile. The choice found as great favour with him as with the child. Very scrupulous, the boy avoided the smallest claim to the name till it should be his by right. "Child" he still remained.

It was on the Feast of St. Luke, a glorious day of the Saint's own summer, that Abbot Hilary gave it to him. He had no mind to keep him waiting over long. Conversant with the main truths of Christianity, their elaboration could come later.

Early in the morning, the day yet barely awake, Brother Francis roused the child, clad him in the white robe of the catechumen. To the east the sky was shot with pearly light. Birds twittered from the bushes in the garden below. The soft air came through the window.

"'Tis your true birthday morning," said Brother Francis smiling, as he led him from the room.

The child was very quiet. You see him humble, trustful; his spirit wrapped in implicit faith. The Unseen World with which he would presently be in communion already enfolded him in its vastness. He felt unconsciously that to which he could assuredly have given no word. Where formerly his soul in bondage to another, possessed by another's will, had striven to storm unlawful heights, and thereby in a measure,—through no actual fault of his own,—had become co-operator with Satanic cunning, now trustful, with full and quiet Act of Faith, it awaited the Divine Gift.

A soft grey light was in the chapel, though night shadows lingered yet in the corners. A faint breath of incense pervaded the place. Man and boy bent the knee in honour of Christ in the Blessed Sacrament, then knelt near the font.

To them came Abbot Hilary. Throughout the ceremony the child held himself very simply. When the holy water touched his forehead, and he heard the words, "*In nomine Patris, et Filii, et Spiritus sancti,*" he fetched a little sigh. Here the assurance of safe harbourage had come to his soul. From thence he could look forward nothing doubting.

Methinks his child's heart sang a Te Deum as presently Brother Francis led him to a pew near the altar that he might hear the Abbot's Mass. Gravely happy he knelt there, seeing the future in a glow of soft light.

With supplication and praise the Mass went forward. At the Elevation of the Sacred Host, Michael raised his head a moment. He could not see the White Disc held high in the Abbot's hands. But, with the inner sight of faith, he saw a Figure standing before the altar, saw the gleaming Robe, the Grave Eyes, and the Wound upon the Generous Hand stretched out to him....

Truly, as Brother Hilary had said, it was his birthday.

CHAPTER XXV

AN ORCHARD EGOIST

WHEN Peregrine left Dieuporte he struck straight through the valley between the wooded slopes of the hills. The autumn morning was very fair, as we have seen. This, added to his recent escape from blackness, lent zest to his spirit. For the first time for many a long month he found his heart going out to Nature. It winged freely to meet her, as a bird escaped from a cage. He welcomed the breath of the wind upon his forehead, he exulted in the sunshine, in the good clean smell of the earth around him.

Extraordinarily light-hearted, he pursued his way, giving gay greeting to peasants as he passed them at cottage doors. The intoxication of the morning caught him; he was drunk with its beauty and brightness. Around him lay orchards aglow with red and russet apples. In one, a girl was standing on a rough ladder, gathering the fruit into a blue apron. As she worked she sang:

"When Autumn brings her goodly store
Of fruit and corn to ev'ry door,
We garner all with care.
Then bird and beast and man always,
Throughout the colder, bleaker days,
The harvesting shall share.

"When Autumn purple, gold, and red,
Brings to us Winter's daily bread
In glowing croft and field,
We bless the rain that watered earth,
The sun that brought the crops to birth,
A gracious store to yield.

"When Autumn bids the brown leaves fall,
When earth half drowsing hears her call
To sleep through Winter days,
We gather all there is of good,

Of earth's most bounteous wholesome food,

Give God the heartfelt praise."

She sang in a low round contralto, a voice as ripe as her beauty. Peregrine, plucking the tabor from beneath his cloak, joined in with the last verse. She turned her head at the sound, gave him a gay good-morning at the end of words and music.

"So you are a musician," quoth she.

"Of a sort," smiled Peregrine.

"No bad sort," she returned with a motherly air which sat well on her. "Sing you to me."

"What should I sing?" demanded Peregrine.

"That which likes you," returned the girl. "We ever perform best that which pleases us most."

Peregrine laughed, and struck a couple of chords on the tabor.

"I see freedom pleasing me most at the moment," he said. And set himself to sing:

"Of all good gifts is freedom more

To man than other good gifts be,

By it he sets most gracious store.

To roam at will o'er hill and lea

Is truly more to him than gold,

Or silver very freely given.

Methinks the heart grows never old

That ne'er has been in thraldom driven.

Who lives in freedom lives at ease,

Knows naught of ill or irksome care.

There's little else a man may please

In freedom's stead; no goodly share

Of oil or wine or golden corn.

Since freedom is both blythe and gay,

And like to earth's most fairest morn,

Of freedom will I sing alway."

His voice died away. The girl looked down upon him.

"A fair song," she said appraisingly, setting her teeth in the side of a red apple. And then she laughed.

"Why do you laugh?" asked Peregrine.

She stretched one arm wide, embracing Nature, as it were.

"Because the day is very good, and because the apple is sweet, and because—because I am alive." She bit again into the apple.

Peregrine eyed her approvingly. "Three most excellent reasons. You find happiness in life?"

"Why not?" quoth she between her munching. "Is it not well to be alive? Does not the sun shine for me, the wind blow for me, the earth bear fruit for me, the birds sing to me? Truly I find happiness in life."

"You envy none?" asked Peregrine.

She laughed. "Whom should I envy? Old Mother Esther down yonder, who has three cows, and is toothless, and has a wart as big as a hazel-nut on her nose? Grizel Burnside, who has a husband who beats her six nights out of the seven, and half a dozen squalling brats tugging at her skirts? Lambert Groot, who they say has a bag of gold pieces he counts the while he yells with rheumatic pains? For my part, I say let Esther keep her cows and her wart and her lack of teeth; Grizel, her husband and her brats; Lambert, his gold and his rheumatism. I am happier with our one cow, my own teeth, my freedom, and my health. I'd barter no jot nor tittle of my own self for all their belongings in a heap at my feet. I am I, and glad on it." An unconscious egoist, she faced him laughing from the ladder.

"Yet," suggested Peregrine, "there are others rich, well-fed, and with good health,—plenty of them in the world. Do you not envy them?"

"Not I," laughed the girl. "How know I that, for all their solid riches, they love the gold of the buttercups in April? that, for all their good feeding, they would pluck and eat blackberries from the hedges along with a juicy apple? that, for all their health they could, race the dewy meadows bare-footed, face the August sun uncovered, or meet a January snow-storm unshrinking. Sooner be myself with the likings I know, than they with tastes more than perchance foreign to me."

"My child," said Peregrine gaily, "I appreciate your confidence in yourself. An' a man have confidence in himself 'twill lead him far."

She looked at him from beneath her eyelashes. "Whither hath it led you?" she asked demurely.

This caused Peregrine a slight inward wince, brought his light statement closer to book. In a sudden flash he saw his words not too wise. Truly may confidence in himself lead a man far, and yet no nearer his goal. Her question, drawn at a venture, shot very near home. Yet he had no mind to betray this thought to the laughing girl.

"Truly," he said airily enough, "at the moment it hath led me to the company of a very fair egoist."

Head on one side she surveyed him, doubtful, questioning. "I know not that word," she said.

"I see it meaning one exceeding conscious of their own personality," remarked Peregrine. "An' you be not conscious of yours, I stand rebuked."

She mused a moment. "An' you mean that I know well that I am Méllisande the Fair, as men call me, that I take pleasure in my beauty and my health, then you need no rebuke."

"Indeed," said Peregrine smiling at her *naïveté*, "I mean that very precisely."

"Then," quoth she, with her ever ready laugh, "the word suits well enough." She dropped to silence a moment; then spoke. "Whither fare you now?"

"I fear me," said Peregrine, "that I fare on a very elusive quest."

"What manner of quest?"

"The quest of a woman."

"Oh!" Méllisande opened dark eyes, braced herself against the ladder. "Tell me more," said she interested.

"There is little enough to tell," returned Peregrine, "and that being so, the quest appears the more mad."

Briefly he gave her the history of the past months, eliminating matter he held undesirable to repeat. She listened, gravely intent.

"I have heard tell of the woman," she said as he came to an end of the story, "veiled, and with quiet eyes."

"You have heard tell of her!" cried Peregrine.

She nodded. "Listen. 'Tis my little brother who has spoken of her. Truly I have thought his words but imagining, since he is a dreamer and over-apt to fancies, at least so I have held. But more than once he has spoken of this woman, and in much the same words that you have given me. Once I thought 'twas the Blessed Virgin he had believed to see, but he assured me to the contrary. This woman, he avows, is purple-robed, her face white as jasmine flowers, and half hidden in a veil; her eyes, when she looks at you, are like moonlit lakes among mountains,—lakes unruffled by the least breath of wind. This is what my brother Aelred has told me."

"Then," said Peregrine very firmly, "I will speak with Aelred."

Méllisande pointed to the right.

"You will find him yonder, most like," she said. "Follow the road through the village, bear upwards along a rocky path, and you will hear the sound of falling water. Make for the sound. A stream comes out of the rock near here, emptying itself into a cup-shaped hollow. 'Tis there where Aelred plays most often, or dreams rather, for he is not over-given to play, being somewhat crippled. Question him gently, and perchance he will tell you more. But he cares not to speak too freely of such matters, since men are apt to mock at him."

"I thank you well," said Peregrine, and turned to go.

"Not too fast," cried Méllisande, "first you must have reward for your song. Hold out your cloak."

Peregrine, laughing, spread out his cloak as bidden. She tossed apples to him till he vowed he could carry no more. Bestowing them about his person, he gave merry thanks.

"Farewell, orchard egoist," he said, "perchance we meet again."

"Who knows!" she nodded. "Fare you well." She saw him depart light-footed. Once again she turned singing to her apples.

CHAPTER XXVI

AELRED'S BELIEF

THE sound of falling water caught on Peregrine's ear as he came to the foot of the small ravine. It was but a faint musical tinkle, since rain had been scarce during the past weeks. His way led him up a narrow pathway, somewhat rough, and steep-rocked on either side. The rocks were covered with stonecrop, a mass of white and yellow flowers earlier in the year; now merely small succulent leaves remained. Here and there grew patches of heather, its flowers likewise gone; only an occasional purple spray lingered among the withered brownness. The sun beat warmly on the path, falling very straight between the rocks.

Before him the way turned right and left, divided by a grass-covered slope. The sound of the falling water brought him to the left. Here the rocks held stunted trees, ash and elder, drawing small sustenance from the sparse earth. Further on the trees thickened, vegetation became more luxurious: now the sound of the water came very clearly to his ear. A moment later a slight bend in the path brought him upon it, a thin silver stream coming from the rocks above, and falling into a cup-shaped hollow.

By the hollow a boy was sitting. Peregrine judged him ten years old or thereabouts. His brown hair was cut straight across his forehead, and at the nape of his neck. He sat very still, his hands clasped round his knees. From afar you might have fancied him sleeping, but for a certain tenseness in his attitude. Coming nearer, you would have seen his eyes open, staring straight before him.

The sound of Peregrine's step on the rocky earth brought him back to matters present. He raised his head quickly, the movement like that of a startled fawn.

Peregrine, coming near the boy, paused. "May I rest awhile?" he asked.

"Indeed, sir," said the boy shyly, "this is no private place."

"Yet courtesy prompts the query," smiled Peregrine, "since I see you first established here."

For answer Aelred moved a wooden crutch. Peregrine sat down by him.

"A very peaceful place," said he, scarce knowing how best to broach the matter he had in mind.

"I like the sound of the falling water," said the boy.

"'Tis musical enough," said Peregrine somewhat absently.

Aelred eyed him frankly. Then with a child's directness put a frank question.

"Are you very weary?"

Peregrine turned. "To speak truth, not weary at all at the moment, though methinks I have known weariness more often than not."

"Yet you are strong," said Aelred wistfully, glancing from the man to his own twisted foot.

"Weariness of body were better to suffer than mind weariness," said Peregrine a trifle bitterly.

Aelred was silent. Here was matter beyond his ken.

"Yet you do not see me weary now," said Peregrine quickly, noting his sorry look.

There fell a silence. He saw not how to lure the boy to speech, fearful lest question should shut his lips beyond chance of opening them. He felt in the child's mind something alert, watchful, ready to hide on the smallest hint of intrusion. He saw not in what fashion he might best make gentle approach. Thus it was he sat silent, listening to the falling water.

Had he known, he could have used no better method of allurement than this very silence. The boy saw himself in a manner a host. He had averred, and truly, this was no private ground, nevertheless it was ground but rarely visited save by him. This gave him in a sense possession of it. It had become his by some inscrutable law of communion with its spirit. An' you are alive to the great elemental forces of Nature, you will find a waiting spirit in all isolated places, ready to welcome or repel according to the kindredship of your soul. Welcomed, you are made lord of the domain by tacit consent. You return again and yet again till it becomes more fully yours by sovereign right. The presence of an intruder is made known to you rather by the resentfulness of the spirit of the place than by any volition of your own.

Aelred found the man beside him no intruder: he knew him for a welcomed guest. Therefore it behooved him to show hospitality. To this end, he broke presently into shy yet courteous speech.

"A thrush nested in yon thorn-bush in the spring. I saw her teach three little ones to fly."

Here came opportunity. They were off in a moment among bird and beast, capping each other with greater marvel as to the ways of the woodland creatures. Aelred found his master in these matters. Ere long he became sole listener, drinking in the man's words with eager ears. Peregrine told him of his own boyish rescuing of the hare from the huntsmen and harriers. Further, of finding, once on a time, a sorely wounded fox cub, of the vixen's moan over it; told of carrying it back to her lair the while she trotted beside him, dog-like in her confidence; told of her jealous guard of it through the days of its mending; and, at the last how he had returned to find her and her young playing before the nest, the once injured cub among them; told how she had picked it from among the rest and laid it at his feet in gratitude, yelping softly with delight the while.

Here was comradeship of taste that brought them to quick understanding. There is none that draws together so quickly or so surely. Anon Peregrine ventured on the matter most present to his mind; spoke briefly of his seeking. He put no question; making his own desire known, he waited. Aelred, having seen a comrade in the man, was quick to give a comrade's aid. His face a-quiver he spoke eagerly.

"Ah, but I have seen her. I know not who she is nor whence she comes. Most often she kneels by me in the church down yonder when I am alone. 'Twas there I first saw her. Once she met me on the hillside. I mind the day well. I was angered since one had spoken ill words to me. Up on the hill I saw the sun setting, and I—I knew it should not go down on anger. So presently I was sorry. Then I saw her coming towards me. It seemed that she came right from the sunset, though 'twas not that truly, but merely that the light was behind her. She looked at me, and called me, "Little Aelred." She touched my forehead, and so left me. I know not whither she went, as I know not whence she comes. But I mind that day very well."

You see him alight, eager, exceeding desirous of making his knowledge of the woman known.

"Then is she no fancy of the brain," said Peregrine softly.

"Indeed no," laughed the boy joyously. "Perchance even now she is down yonder. Truly I have seen her there full oft."

Here was very definite assurance. The whole simplicity of it held him silent. For months he had wandered heart sick in pursuit. Now he found himself almost in her presence, and at the moment when, for all his vaunted words to Abbot Hilary, he had found himself nigh on abandoning the quest, turning for satisfaction to Nature and her varying moods. He saw himself a coward for his doubt: knew more certainly his great desire to come to her presence. I do not think he dwelt vastly now, no more than formerly, on what the meeting should bring him. It was enough to know she was no dream. An' he could come to full assurance on this score, 'twere joy enough. The boy brought to words what trembled in his mind.

"An' we went now to the church, we might find her there."

Peregrine got to his feet; lifted the boy from the ground, adjusted the crutch beneath his arm.

"Come," he said briefly.

They set out adown the rocky path. Peregrine found it none too easy work to curb his steps to the boy's halting pace. His heart made haste before him, went eager to the desired meeting. He doubted not for one instant he should find her there. Long sought, long desired, he would see her face to face.

The village appeared deserted; the inhabitants within doors were partaking of the noonday meal. The sun lay golden on the roadway. Anon, before him, he saw the grey church, the porch shadowed by a great yew tree. Aelred's crutch tapped softly up the flagged path. Together they entered the door.

The place was cool and dusky, smelling faintly of incense and candle fumes. A great Crucifix hung above the Rood Loft, dimly discernible in the shadows overhead. The Pyx Light shone soft and red.

They looked round: saw the building empty. Disappointment fell cold to Peregrine's heart. Aelred lifted a reassuring face.

"Anon she may come," he whispered. "Shall we wait and pray."

"Pray you an' you will," said Peregrine somewhat coldly, "I will bide here."

He stood within the doorway, arms folded. He had no mind to bend the knee. Ancient memories were hotly astir within him. Age-old custom, or something stronger, called loudly to him: pride mocked at the call.

Aelred limped up the aisle; made for a bench on his right. Here he came to his knees, while Peregrine watched motionless. An' she passed not him to enter, she must needs come by a small door by the Lady Chapel. His eyes for the most part on this, though now and again turning to the kneeling boy, he waited. The minutes passed leaden-footed. At length Aelred got up from his knees.

Very sick at heart, Peregrine came through the porch, and into the sunlight. There he awaited the boy. Aelred came towards him, his face radiant.

"You saw her!" he cried.

Peregrine stared. "I saw her!" he echoed dumbfounded.

"She came even as I knelt," he said joyous. Then stopped, struck mute by the sight of the man's face.

"Ah, what is it?" he asked on a note almost piteous.

"Bah!" laughed Peregrine mockingly. "I might have known it but a figment of the brain. Yet that a child should be deceived!"

"What mean you?" asked Aelred trembling.

"There was no one near you." He shot forth the words bitterly. Then turning strode away.

White-faced the boy looked after him.

CHAPTER XXVII

THE RECLUSE

AN' you knew Greatoak Forest,—a vast place and well named by reason of its trees,—you might perchance have heard rumour of its recluse. Men spoke of him as a tall man, clad in a white woollen garment, feeding on roots and berries, and in league with mysterious powers.

This was but half truth, as such rumours are like to be. That he was a tall man may be safely accorded; that he wore a white woollen garment fashioned after the manner of a sleeved cloak, and girt about the waist with a leathern belt, may be also accorded. Given these two matters, further rumour was not over accurate. Forest roots and berries he would have found poor sustenance for his muscular body. He gained better nourishment from the wheat and vegetables he grew in the ground around his cabin; from snared rabbits, dressed and seasoned with herbs and onions. At leaguing with mysterious powers he would have laughed frankly and very truly. Nature was the goddess he worshipped, and he saw in her an all-sufficient mistress.

In body he was tall and muscular, as you have seen. In face he was dark and sunburned, having something of a foreign mien. Black hair covered his head; his eyes, grey and far-seeing, looked straight upon the world unflinching. Clear eyes they were, having the look of seeing more than was physically apparent. They would gaze at you very frankly after the manner of a man who has nothing to hide, and yet you found yourself no nearer knowledge of the mind of the gazer in meeting them. No doubt this last lent a hand in giving colour to the rumour of mystery, though truly that he was seldom seen beyond the forest was mystery enough for peasant folk. Your coarser man dwells willingly in herds, save when he is injured. Then it is his instinct to creep away from sight after the manner of some wounded beast.

Oswald was his name: and Oswald the Recluse men called him. He was seldom seen, as I have told you. Now and again men had glimpses of him, this at dawn or sunset, walking some distant hillside. Boys penetrating the depths of the forest in search of birds' nests brought back word of him sitting by his cabin door, very still and silent. Yet none ventured within distance of discovery by him; or fancied they did not. Had they guessed at the alert mind within the still body, they had known their presence less hidden than they fondly imagined.

It disturbed him no more than the scampering of a squirrel up a tree, or the rustle of a dormouse among dried leaves. These brown-faced youngsters, peering shyly curious from among bush and bracken, were to him but part and parcel of the great stream of Nature's life around him. They were young enough to have no conscious separation from it. They took hunger and sleepiness in the natural course of things, neither denying the one nor combating the other. He saw in them merely young animals, unselfconscious though shy of the unknown: in this case of himself. It was with your grown man that, for the most part, he knew himself in lack of sympathy; those who neither consciously nor unconsciously accept Nature as their mistress, nor see their own lordship of her: those who grumble and carp at her decrees, master neither of her nor of themselves.

In this mastery alone he saw full freedom of spirit. I have told you that he worshipped Nature; that she was his mistress. This is true. But it was the worship a man gives to the woman who is his mate as well as his goddess; who knows himself her lord even while he does her willing homage.

One night, standing before his cabin door, he surveyed the stars. The air was still and frosty: the quiet of the sleeping forest lay around him. This was the hour he felt his own most fully; himself awake, alive, while Nature slept. Even the trees were wrapt to slumber, very motionless, their bare branches darkly outlined against the luminous sky. There was no moon: among the brighter stars the Milky Way flung her whitely powdered track, a far-off illimitable path. Immensity around him, his soul winged dauntless out to it.

Suddenly he came back to earth, very alert, on the scent of an intruder. You would have declared all around to be silent, still as the grave: Oswald stood with head bent, listening intently. The minutes passed: from far off came the lightest stirring of the undergrowth, a mere rustle as of the faintest breath of wind. Muscles tensioned, Oswald raised his head, looked towards the place whence the sound had come. Now it grew more distinct; there was the snapping of a twig. Suddenly from among the trees stepped a tall man, dark-cloaked. The two confronted each other, hostile for the moment.

Oswald broke the silence, since truly it behooved one of them to break it.

"Who are you?" he asked, putting the most natural question, and the one that came readiest to his tongue.

"One, Peregrine," replied the intruder. "Truly an' you are surprised to see me, which I take it you be, I am none less surprised to see you. Are you spirit or mortal?"

"Very much mortal," returned Oswald laughing. "And mortal enough to be frankly startled by your appearance. I look not for wayfarers so far afield, and at this hour."

Peregrine gazed around him. In the moonlight he saw the cabin; a rough place enough, built of logs and wattles.

"You live here?" he asked wondering.

"I do. An' you would have rest and shelter you are welcome to what I can offer you."

"I accept your offer gladly," said Peregrine. "I have walked far enough for the nonce,—over far for that matter."

"Then the sooner you come to a halt the better," returned Oswald. And he led the way within the cabin.

For all its roughness it was clean and freshsmelling, holding a scent of peat, bracken, and dried herbs, which latter dangled in bunches from a string across one corner. A peat fire lighted the place dimly, flinging great shadows on the log walls.

"Sit you there," said Oswald, pointing to a heap of bracken; and forthwith busied himself with the preparation of food.

Ere long he had it ready,—crushed corn mixed with goat's milk and boiled to a smooth paste, sweetened with honey. He ladled it steaming from an iron pot into two bowls fashioned from the dried and seasoned rind of a pumpkin. Peregrine wolfed it down; you could see he brought hunger to it as a very excellent sauce. For drink, Oswald made a beverage from herbs of his own gathering, a dark brew but not unpalatable. Anon, filled and rested, Peregrine gave vent to a great sigh.

"That," he said, "was exceeding welcome. You saw me pretty near the end of my tether."

Oswald nodded. "So I fancied. You had been journeying long?"

"It's five months or thereabouts since I found myself beneath a roof. You lose track of time with naught but the look of the fields to guide you."

"An' you trust to so scant guidance you may find yourself sadly astray," returned Oswald. "I keep count with these tallies." He lifted a bundle of twelve hazel rods from a corner. One was notched the whole length, another but half way.

"From your marking I judge us to be now near the middle of February," said Peregrine eyeing the bundle.

"You judge correctly; the sixteenth day to be accurate."

"I had thought it earlier."

"That is where your mere observation of the fields makes bad guess-work, since the weather has a hand in the reckoning," quoth Oswald calmly. "Take to my method. A tally a month will suffice you to carry around, and a notch in the outer side of the next one to mark the casting away of the last."

"No bad idea," returned Peregrine. And a silence fell.

Oswald watched him. He was quick to read slight tokens anywhere, whether of character in a man's face, or the hint of weather's change in sky, wind, or flower. He saw him a man not wholly content with life, yet not fully aware of the fact himself. He saw in him something of an anomaly,—a dreamer without a dream, a traveller without a goal. This is unsatisfactory an' Nature has made of you a dreamer; Fate, or yourself, thrust you forth to travel.

"Whither were you faring when you chanced on this place?" he asked presently.

"Nowhere," returned Peregrine. "Once having a goal in view, which I found on nearer approach to be pure moonshine, I sought no other. I wander now where fancy leads me."

Oswald shook his head. "Fancy is too moody a jade for my guide. At times she leads in hot haste with no consideration for him who follows. At times she stays moping, forcing a man to idle in one spot at her will."

At this Peregrine demurred. "I see her will and mine in accord," quoth he.

Oswald laughed, denying the argument firmly. "You may think so, but 'tis not the case. An' you take her for guide, you have no will in the matter, or rather, make it subservient to hers. An' a man use his own will, he makes a slave of fancy." He paused a moment, then continued. "How know you your goal mere moonshine? Did you gain it?"

"Near enough to know it non-existent, naught but a fancy of the brain."

Oswald moved impatiently. "There you are back at your fancy. I told you she was no good guide."

"In this case she was not of my own seeking."

"You speak in riddles," said Oswald. "You may think me over-blunt, but, if a man speak in riddles, methinks he has little to tell. Fact will bear plain words and close handling."

Peregrine looked at him. He was not displeased with his bluntness. He saw in him one who came to a grip with matters. Mayhap, he lost hold on a part of what he gripped at, since a man's grasp is not over-large; nevertheless he saw him making sure of what he grasped.

"You shall have the story plainly," said Peregrine. And forthwith gave it to him.

On the conclusion Oswald made no answer, but remained half-musing. When at last he spoke it was as though he conferred with himself.

"I too have had glimpse of the woman you seek. I, too, sought her, moved Heaven and Earth and Hell to that end, and came no nearer finding her. Now frankly, I know not whether she is mortal or spirit. This much I know truly: she is no fancy as you have said. Spirit she may be, and probably is, though I still give the benefit of the doubt to her mortal nature,—if the doubt be benefit. Of that I am none too sure. This further conclusion I have come to also; she is not to be found for all our seeking. An' she come again willingly,—mortal or spirit,—as she came once in glimpse, 'twill be her affair, not ours. For my part, I dwell in my memory of her. That she is existent suffices me. I seek no further knowledge of her save at her own will." He stopped. Then a moment later he continued. "I see her eyes in the moonlit pools of the forest; her purple veil in the spreading of the twilight; her presence in the quiet of the night. This much my momentary sight of her has given me, and for the gift I am thankful."

"Then you hold the sight no illusion?" asked Peregrine.

"None," said Oswald calmly. "I will put the matter plainly. An' a blind man be restored to sight at sundown, he may get a glimpse of the sun as it sinks behind the hills. The morning may dawn cloudy; and throughout the day, and even succeeding days, he may get no sight of its further glory. But it was no illusion that he had seen it, and will see it again when the clouds disperse. But he can have no more hand in dispersing the clouds, than he can have in changing the course of the sun behind them. There's the matter as I take it. You may journey the length and breadth of the world, and come no nearer her. You must wait her own coming again."

Peregrine thought awhile; found a certain solace in Oswald's words. At length he spoke.

"Yet the boy saw her. And I, though present, saw her not."

"That bears out my thought that she is spirit," said Oswald, "but does not prove her fancy. Though doubtless you rubbed illusion well into the child's mind."

Peregrine was silent. Shame struck on him.

"Having ever held her purely material you were like to do so," said Oswald calmly. "You were less actually blameworthy than over precipitate. Since I hold her to be spirit you were probably beyond the range of sight of her. I do not say this of a surety since I hold that sight of her comes at her will rather than ours; but I do say, that had man or child given me as great proof of knowledge of her as yon child gave you, I had followed most closely in his steps, seen eye to eye with him as near as might be. On your own showing you stood far from him."

Peregrine was still silent. He felt himself more than fool.

Oswald eyed him kindly. "Do not be downcast, man. There's no mother's son of us but blunders once—aye, often more than once, and that, perchance, within a foot of our goal. Recognizing that, there's humiliation to add to the wounds and fatigue of the journey. This, bringing discouragement, makes acquiescence in failure the easier course. 'Tis the coward's outlook. Face the matter again. In this case I say, take courage; believe in her, and await her coming."

The words brought comfort to Peregrine. He looked gratefully at his mentor. You might have seen trust in his eyes. The personality and confidence of the man gave him strength.

"An' you take my advice," said Oswald, "you will sleep now. New hope comes with the morning."

He showed him a bed of bracken, made him lie down. Then himself laid down at the other side of the cabin.

It was long before Peregrine slept. Thoughts pursued each other pell-mell through his brain, one alone predominant and lasting enough to grasp, namely, that in his host he had found comprehension of the matter that absorbed him, and sanity combined. This thought at length brought him rest. An hour or so before daybreak he slept.

CHAPTER XXVIII

IN THE FOREST

MORNING brought refreshment, and with it new hope and courage as Oswald had foretold. At breakfast he put a proposal to Peregrine frankly enough.

"An' you are so minded, why not bide with me a time. Men term me a recluse, and so in a measure I am, finding little congenial in the majority of mankind. I should find no constraint in your presence. We could talk when the mood was on us, and—better test of congeniality—keep silence when we willed. Have you mind to try the partnership for a while?"

Peregrine gave willing assent. Already, as seen, he had found rest in the man's confidence, a healthfulness in his quiet sanity. He saw a haven in the forest cabin, one where he would abide most gladly. To have no fear of going a day, or even more, hungry was something of a novelty to him. The search for food sharpens a man's wits with regard to attaining the necessities of life, but leaves less room for the development of other faculties. Here was sufficient for the needs of the body. His mind at rest on this score, it began to expand in other directions. His love of Nature returned to him, as it had returned for a brief space on his leaving Dieuporte. In this renewal of his love he realized how long it had been absent.

Tracing his way slowly backwards, he came to the point where the love had first waned; saw it in his absorption in the human, namely Isabel. Up to this point there had been freedom of spirit; here he first saw his bondage, realized himself enslaved; slave of the woman at Belisle; slave of luxury at Castle Syrtes; slave of Menippus; and, lastly, slave of an idea. In this last he was, however, none so certain of the bondage; of the former slavery he was very sure.

Now he felt his spirit free. The intimacy of Nature again surrounded him; he found sweetness in her breath; in her still, sunny days, despite their cold; in her frosty, starlit nights. He found himself watching the brown buds slowly swelling on the trees, gazing with something akin to reverence at the first pale primrose lifting a shy face among last year's withered débris, touching the tiny fragile flower of the wood sorrel. The clean healthiness of the forest absorbed him; his spirit was at one with the tender life awaking around him.

A new idea came to him now. Up to a point he acquiesced with Oswald in the thought that the woman would make herself known to them at her own time; yet he saw himself fitting his spirit for the meeting. In this he believed himself in a measure seeking her. You see him humble; no longer hot afoot to the chase in his own way, striving to attain to her by the force of his own will. He never for an instant lost sight on the thought of her. Now and again he fancied her eyes watching him; prayed her then humbly enough to make her presence known at her own time.

Oswald, half laughing, told him he held her so close in thought no sight of her was needed to him now. To which Peregrine replied briefly:

"Belief in her may be good; but sight of her will be better."

In his belief he now surpassed his one-time mentor. He looked daily,—even momentarily,—to her appearance, where Oswald was content to leave it at months or even years ahead. It was sufficient to him that she existed. The mere knowledge, without perpetual watching, was not enough for Peregrine.

He saw too great passivity of mind in Oswald. Though in a measure he recognized its excellence, his own spirit was a-tingle for greater action. The man's quiet certainty of the woman's existence was at once an anodyne and an irritant to him. While Oswald's belief quickened his own belief, he yet saw something lukewarm in his lack of action. This Oswald guessed at, rather by intuition than by actual spoken word from Peregrine. For his part, he saw a certain weakness in Peregrine's constant expectancy. He watched him walking alert in the forest, his eyes roving from side to side.

"I have told you," he said once quietly, "that effort on your part is useless. She will come at her own time."

"Truly you say so," returned Peregrine, "and at the first I had confidence in your assurance. Now, I know not fully how to make my meaning clear; but to my thinking she bids me still seek her; awaits a further effort on my part."

Oswald smiled. "There imagination has you in thrall. On your own showing you have pursued her long without avail. Rest in her spirit which you know around you, and await sight of her quietly as I do. Your constant expectancy of her coming brings disquietude to your mind."

Reasonable enough argument, and yet one which Peregrine could not bring himself fully to accept.

"Look at the matter dispassionately," said Oswald. "You dreamed the existence of this woman. Knowing not whether the dream were truth or reality, you pursued her for over two years. The pursuit brought with it disappointment, and worse. Now I tell you of a certainty your dream was true, and show you the means by which the truth shall become fact to you.

In seeking her, in your constant watching for her, you drive her from you. I know not why this is so; nevertheless I know it to be true."

Peregrine was silent. Here was apparent certainty presented to him on the one hand; as the pull against it was his own inner conviction, which he had yet more than once proved illusion, so it seemed. For the time he let the matter be; came again to rest in the strength of his comradeship, and the sweetness of Nature round him.

So the days passed. March came with strong clean winds blowing through the forest, with daffodils tossing golden heads by brook-sides, a very wealth of gladness. With her passing came quieter April bringing sunshine and rain, and the scent of growing things in the forest. The birds mated and sang; the whole place was alive and buoyant.

One night Peregrine awakened suddenly. At the first waking he fancied Oswald to have called to him, but his quiet regular breathing showed him sleeping. Peregrine raised himself on his elbow and looked around.

The faintest grey light fell through the square opening which served as window. He sank back prepared for further sleep, when on a sudden he found himself more fully awake. He sat up, and again looked round the hut. The bunches of herbs dangling from their string looked ghostly in the grey light. Oswald, lying on a bed of bracken, slept soundly.

Peregrine got up from his couch, donned his clothes, barely conscious that he did so. His mind was busily astir; though as yet his thoughts had found no conscious articulation. Being clad, he took a chunk of bread from a shelf. This much he knew his host would have freely given him. Then he moved softly to the door, opened it.

The forest lay in the quiet which reigns most supremely betwixt night and dawn. For some moments he stood looking towards the great trees, then stepped without, closed the door softly behind him.

Now, an' you were to ask me for reasons as to why Peregrine left the hut at this very moment, I must e'en tell you frankly that where fifty instincts urged him to the move there was no one definite reason. This may seem folly; but verily, to my thinking, there are moments in a man's life when he does better to obey the lightest instinct than the closest reasoning. We are come now to a time in our Jester's wanderings when I see myself penning that which actually befell him, rather than the thoughts which led him to action. It may be that you will guess at those thoughts, having had some such of your own. An' you cannot trace them in his actions, I see not any words of mine setting them clearly before you.

Having put some half-dozen miles or so between himself and the hut, he began to feel sleepy. Coming to a mossy stretch beneath a great oak, he lay down. Three minutes saw him wrapped in slumber, and he slept soundly.

When he awakened it was high noon. The sun fell through the oak branches, clear upon the place where he lay. For a time longer he rested, revelling in the warmth of its beams. Anon he sat up; ate a portion of the bread he had brought with him. All around him was intensely still. Before him were massed bluebells, a soft luminous carpet. Brilliant nearer him, they lost themselves anon in the hazy distances among the trees. He sat a while gazing at them.

He wandered through the forest that day; at night made it his resting-place.

CHAPTER XXIX

EASTER EVE AND EASTER MORNING

EARLY the next morning Peregrine was again afoot. Coming at length from among the trees, he found himself on a hillside. Below him was a hamlet, a small cluster of some dozen or so cottages nestling at the foot of the hill. Later, an' he would, he might seek food at one of them; at the moment he had bread sufficient to stay hunger, and had little mind to find himself again in the company of men.

Partly descending the hill, he sat down beneath a thorn-bush, looking on the landscape spread below him. Sounds of life came to him on the quiet air; here was the clarion note of a cock, the bark of a dog, the lowing of cows, and the tinkle of a bell at the neck of some goat.

The time passed pleasantly enough beneath the thorn-bush. He found himself in no mood to desert his post. Dreamily he watched the shifting lights and shadows in the valley, and on the hills beyond.

The sound of footsteps brought him again to the present. He looked up. Almost opposite to him were a boy and girl, the boy ten years old or thereabouts, the girl some three years younger. Her brown hair was covered with a purple hood; a dress of the same colour fell to her ankles; a white kerchief was folded about her neck; her arms were full of bluebells. The boy, a sturdy fellow, clad in green tunic and hose, and having a brown cap on his head, held a great sheaf of cherry blossom. Peregrine straightway thought of Pippo.

Coming to a halt they gazed at him, round-eyed, astonished at the sight of a stranger.

"Good-day," quoth Peregrine smiling at their astonishment.

"Good-day," echoed the boy. The girl remained mute; a very shy maiden.

"You are well laden," said Peregrine.

The boy glanced at his burden. "We take them to the church yonder." He nodded leftwards up the hill.

Peregrine half turned; saw what had before escaped his notice, a small grey church on the hillside, set on the edge of the forest.

"You carry a fair tribute thither," quoth he.

"'Tis Easter Eve," said the boy bluntly.

"Oh!" breathed Peregrine. The syllable showing him ignorant of the fact, the children eyed him puzzled. How should the passing of the Solemn Week have escaped him unobserved? This is what their glances asked, though they found no words.

"She takes bluebells," said the boy, nodding towards the girl. "She says Christ must surely love them, since they are the colour of His Mother's robe. I climbed for my cherry blossom."

Here Peregrine saw Pippo again. His mouth curved to smile, though memory brought a lurking sadness to his eyes.

Finding no further speech come handy, the boy turned to the girl.

"Come," he said. "Father Felix bade us be betimes."

Together they wended their way up the hillside. Peregrine looked after them, and towards the church.

The sun had fallen behind the forest, leaving it purple-blue against a rosy sky toning upwards to lilac and grey. The air was alive and fragrant with the breath of spring. A thrush sang in an elm tree set close against the church.

Father Felix was sitting on a bench in front of a cottage door. This was the priest's house, and was hard by the church. Since you have met Father Felix before, though in other guise, I refrain from present description of him. His eyes, looking towards the reflection from the sunset, reflected something of its calm. You see him musing on matters well loved by him.

Anon bringing his eyes from the sky, a thought nearer earth, he became aware of a tall man standing near him. Looking at him, he saw in him a stranger.

"I give you good-evening, sir," he said.

"Good-evening," responded Peregrine.

"You are, I fancy, a stranger in these parts," said Father Felix.

"I am," returned Peregrine briefly.

Here conversation seemed like to come to a halt. A frank response with nothing added to it brings matters to a greater standstill than a shifty answer will bring them. The last case leaves room for probing; the first makes further query appear sheer curiosity.

Father Felix surveyed him with kindly blue eyes; Peregrine returned the glance with eyes no less blue.

"Have you come from far?" asked Father Felix, blinking towards the sunset reflection in the eastern sky. Yet, for all his blinking, methinks he saw a good deal.

"Recently from the forest," said Peregrine. "I have been dwelling there some weeks past."

The old man smiled. "Then you are a bit of a hermit like myself. Will you not be seated?" He moved slightly on the bench; at the same time indicated a tree stump near him, thereby giving a choice of seats. Peregrine chose the tree stump.

"And before the forest?" asked Father Felix. "That is if you will see interest rather than curiosity in my queries?"

"Before the forest I was a wanderer," returned Peregrine. Then he pushed back the hood of his cloak, threw it somewhat from his shoulders. "You see in me an outcaste fool." There was a faint ring of challenge in the words.

"Hmm," mused Father Felix gently, his eyes twinkling. "A fool by whose standard? An outcaste from what company? Methinks there lies the test as to whether the title with which you have branded yourself may not be a badge of glory rather than of shame."

Peregrine looked straight before him. "A fool by the standard of men, and by mine own. An outcaste from the Court where I played the fool."

"Since you judge yourself a fool by your own standard, you are assuredly in the way of becoming something greater," said Father Felix quietly. "For the standard of men, I pay not over much heed to that measure when applied to their fellow-mortals. As to the matter of outcaste," he looked at him very straightly, "an' you be not outcaste from God, I see in the business less of a boggle than you perchance see."

"An' I were an outcaste from Him?" queried Peregrine very low.

"Then, my son, the quicker you set about returning to Him the better," quoth Father Felix briskly.

A silence fell on these words. If Peregrine had answer to make it was at the moment no verbal one. The old man having said his say let the matter bide. The light in the sky faded, cooled to a pale blue-grey very restful to contemplate. A star came out over the forest. Big and luminous it hung in the clear space.

Anon Peregrine roused himself.

"I bid you good-evening," he said.

The old man looked at him, seemed about to speak, checked the words on his lips, gave "Good-evening" in response. Peregrine went down the hill.

Coming again to the thorn-bush, he halted irresolute, made half turn to retrace his steps. He denied the impulse; sat down once more beneath the thorn-bush.

Night crept slowly onward, spreading her dusky mantle over the valley. At the foot of the hills it was intensely dark, yet with a soft darkness as of velvet. The night itself was softly velvet; grey velvet above the hills, star-sprinkled. Sirius faced him in a dip between them, blinking now fire-red, now green. No moon being visible, the stars shone with a greater radiance.

Around and about him was intense silence. The earth was caught to slumber. Himself wakeful, he sat immovable, motionless as the thorn-bush by which he rested. His spirit winged into the vast spaces, ranged in circles, returning ever to one point. Staying a moment there, it went forth again, sent by his own will, since he was reluctant to allow it permission to this resting-place.

At length his spirit grew weary of the flight. "I have sought," she said to him, "and here is my sole haven. Let me rest now." Here, clearly, were the words she spoke. How send her forth again upon a barren errand? How bid her seek fruitlessly afar that which lay so near to hand? His will withdrew from the guarded sanctuary. Wings folded, his spirit came to harbourage.

The night wore on. A pale light in the east heralded the coming dawn. He rose from beneath the thorn-bush, turned up the hill.

Within the church was nearly utter darkness; only the one red light glowed as it glows wherever Christ reigns hidden in the Sacred Host.

Father Felix rose from near the altar, came down the aisle to meet him. His eyes were heavy with foregone sleep, yet bright with an immense happiness.

"I was waiting for you," he said.

An hour later Peregrine knelt before the flower-decked altar. Through the open door of the church the dawn showed purple beyond the hills. The sun, coming up above them, shot golden beams into the place, falling upon the Crucifix set among bluebells and snow-white cherry blossom.

Peregrine raised his head. Kneeling near him he saw the Woman he had sought, looked straight into her deep eyes.... For all his joy in her presence it was submerged in the knowledge of One Who had brought him to sight of her.

Father Felix, turning from the door of the sacristy, looked momentarily at the kneeling man. Beyond him, he saw the sun risen above the blue hills.

THE END.

Milton Keynes UK
Ingram Content Group UK Ltd.
UKHW042114220324
439862UK00004B/430